The One True

☐ **Saint Obamas MomJeans** !iOExqqM85g (ID: GnhOG5LT) 08/07/16(Sun)12:02:57 No.84481388 ▶ >>84481557
File: 1465169889588.jpg (189 KB, 436x600)

>>84480990
This Church of Kek is fake!!! Beware imposters. Sacellum Kekellum is the One True Church of Kek!
www.sacellumkekellum.org

Check 'em
Kek has spoken

Saint Obamas Momjeans

ISBN-13: 978-1542770514

ISBN-10: 1542770513

2017 (((K))) Saint Obamas Momjeans LLC

Kekright
Reprint what you like

All OC: Saint Obamas Momjeans
All Copypasta: Anonymous

Contains the following books:

The Divine Word of Kek
Shadilay, My Brothers: Esoteric Kekism & You!
Deus Kek: The Kek & The Dead
Intermediate Meme Magic
Advanced Meme Magic

All available in full color in print and on Kindle

The Divine Word of Kek

Saint Obamas Mom Jeans

THE DIVINE WORD OF KEK

Saint Obamas MomJeans

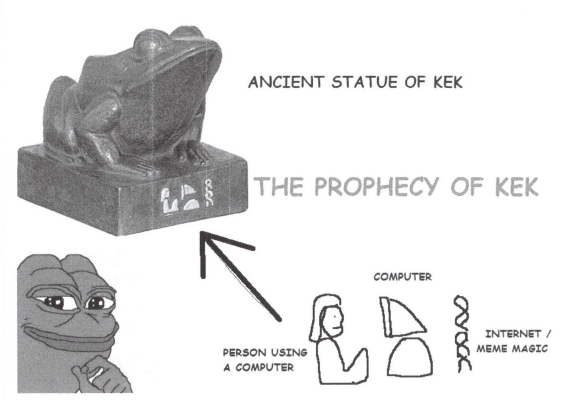

The Chaos Prayer:

O' Kek;
Shamer of Singles
Deliverer of Doubles
Tyrant of Trips
Queen of Quads,
Please bless this post with Meme Magic
And twist reality around the memes we make.

excerpt from the Egyptian "Book of the Dead"

Kek and Keket - Human beings having the heads of Frogs

MEME MAGIC IS REAL

Ring-a-ring-a-Kek,
A pocket full of Happenings;
Ashes! Ashes!
We all fall to Kek.

>>76131555
KEK IS UPON US.

>>76131605
Me to. Actually believing now.

Gonna start creating a KEK folder, to offer him sacrafises, in the form of .jpgs.

>>76132811
We should sacrifice the .jpegs on the new moon probably.

NEW MOON = 5th JUNE FROM 03:59 GMT

SACRIFICE .YOUR .JPGS

TO LORD KEK

Meme up the Kek

Meme it up
While your /pol/ are comfy
And the meme is happening
Look ahead, the crowd is dubbin'

The Kekronomicon:

The Book of Kek

Frater 7777

Genesis
Chapter 1

Before existence, there was Kek. In the vast expansive nothingness of limitless Chaos, Kek slumbered in a state of simultaneous being and non-being. When Ra sprang out of the Chaos and created the universe, Kek awoke in a wrathful state. He knew that the physical creation of Ra was an abomination and something that should not have been.

Kek saw Ra's creation and realized that he must somehow return creation back to the Primordial Chaos. From that point on, he vowed to instill mischief and trickery into the minds of the inhabitants of Ra's creation. Through them, the chosen ones, Chaos would spread throughout creation, breaking the laws of Ma'at and heralding the return of Isfet.

To further disrupt the order of Ra's creation, Kek decided to create a form of his own. The new Chaos-Creation was called the Meme. Through the promulgation of the Meme, Kek's chaotic powers would grow. It would allow his followers and chosen few to experience his formless, senseless, non-existence in a physical way. Because of the Meme, his first followers presented his physical image as taking the shape of a green frog. This physical representation of him would continue throughout time in various civilizations, cultures, and periods.

Memetic Magic

Manipulation of the Root Social Matrix and The Fabric of Reality

KEK, when the letters are composited together, resembles the double-helix pattern of DNA.

Meme it up a little more

Get the party happenin' on the Kek floor
See, 'cause that's where the Kek's at
And you'd find out if you do that

I don't want
A place to praise
Get your memes on the floor tonight
Make His day
I don't want
A place to praise
Get your memes on the floor tonight
Make His day

Praise lord Kek, Lord of light most wise and gracious, open my eyes Kek lead me from the conspirators and their manipulation, strike them down with their own evil and free your followers from their damnat ions!

Kekus Maximus

Holy!
From here I direct my bhakti to
Naught
With each vital organ trembling
At the sound of my vibrating prayer
of Death

Holy!
Burning in frenzy I raise my voice
Turning in for each limb, each dark
Name of Power
I summon, I chant, I pray for
Salvation
Lifeless Redemption
I burn, and I burn, and I burn with
devotion
Death Inebriation

Meme Magic

Meme Magic (or meme magick) is a phenomenon that happens when autistic neckbeards from the internets pool their mana to meme a macro image into reality.
Until this day a number of impressive happenings have been caused using this method.

Origins

The term "meme magic" was first used on 4chan in Summer 2014 by some horsefuckers. Later in Fall 2014 it was mentioned a few times too when Ebola-chan expressed her love to niggers.

Spread

However, in the end it was the cripplechanners who made the term popular because they are obviously betterchan. During the Germanwings crash in Spring 2015 /bane/posters had the feeling that they used meme magic to crash this plane with no survivors. Only a few weeks later new boards that were fully devoted to meme magic (like /bmw/ and /magick/) popped up. Posters started to see their meme magick behind any major happening. Notable examples of those include:

- Ibbi Pipi AKA Ebin Pepe
- Can't stump the Trump
- Ooga Booga Bix Nood
- God Kek

In January 2016 meme archeologists over at cripplechan were surprised to find out that their iconic smug frog is in fact an ancient Edgyptian god who in fact predicted all this autistic nonsense.

So do you want to be a wizard? to change reality collectively.

We can all agree that collective conscious effort can change reality. The /bane/ thoughtform brought down an entire plane from only the collective strength of shitposts?

Can thought really transform reality in such a way that it crashes a plane with no survivors?

Are you ready to accept the greater reality?

All that's required is a few moments of your time. This is enough to change not only your own life, but the life of all 8chan users.

I will unleash easy to follow and usable guidelines that you can follow to channel anything into physical reality. Collectively we can bring any thought into this reality.
The proof has always been right in front of your nose. You just need to try it.

Thoughtforms~

Let's take a moment to remember Ebola-Chan. She is what we would call a thoughtform. Thoughtforms are thought given an "astral" form. The astral world can change physical reality and vice verca.
But what if we could direct what we wanted our thoughtforms to do? To control and summon them into this world.
In step two I'm not only going to teach you the fundamentals of thoughtforms. But how to create them and decide what you want them to do. This will be taught among mong many other magical practices that will change our reality.

Thoughtforms

Every single thought you think creates an astral form. Except most of your thoughts will perish within seconds of creation. So instead let's learn how to collectively create a proper lasting being. First step is the idea. Every thoughtform needs a starting idea or objective (Ebola-Chan's objective was to spread the ebola virus). I'm not going to be giving more examples because any idea you can think of is possible to turn into a thoughtform nomtter what it is or what it does. It can even just be a glorified sex doll.

Second step is to form the body of the thoughtform. Start to visualize a fog of energy in your mind which is absorbing not only your energy but the idea you are giving it. Vocaly speak to this form and tell the ball of energy what you want it to do or what the thoughtforms purpose is.

With proper visualization abilities you will be able to give your thoughtform an astral form of your choosing, human, pony, alien, animal, etc.

Extra information. Giving your thoughtform a name is advisable. Expecially if you are going to be collectively working on it. Also giving your thoughtform a sigil is suggestible since this allows for easy connection to the egregore. As we see Ebola-Chan's sigil is the head piece symbol.

Feeding your thoughtform. Just like humans, thoughtforms require energy to grow big and powerful. Emotion is the most easily transferable energy source. Summon your thoughtform in imagination and start to conjure up emotions of love or lust, gratitude or anger. This will be transfered by imaginative visualization. You can also plan group fap sessions with your board. Thinking of the thoughtform or its sigil while performing energy exchanges will feed it in this manner.

More information on thoughtforming and sigils

Trace, gnosis, theta brainwave state

You might of heard some of these words before. Essentially for all magical practices you are required to enter a deep meditative state. This can be aquired from 5-10 minutes of focusing on your breath and slowly breathing deeply. I advice you to do this before any practice to smooth out visualization and bring more power to your rituals.

Back to thoughtforms

Your thoughts hold power. Emotion is the key to igniting and fueling these thoughts. The more people contributing emotion and energy, the stronger these will become. So collectively you can achive great feats.

Let's talk a little more on the sigil of your thoughtform. Think of these like a symbolic portal to connecting with the egregore. Once the egregore sigil has been created, your group can all enter a collective state of gnosis, stare at the sigil and then channel direct emotion into it. This could include feeling utmost love for your creation, or even a group fap with everying staring at it. The rules are any directed emotion.

Evocation/Summoning

Evocation is the act of connecting ritualistically to your thoughtform. This will allow you to enter direct conversation with the thoughtform. You may ask it questions and even command it to perform your desires. To evocate a spirit or egregore, first draw or print of the sigil(preferably do this with a black marker). Next enter a state of gnosis, you should see tv static. Stare into the sigil untill the lines start to glow or vibrate. Your vision might fog up. Speak the egregores name and ask it to come "come Ebola-Chan, come Ebola-Chan". Repeat this for a minute untill you feel you have made sufficient contant. This is very easy but due to the subtle nature of it you probably wont think you've contacted it(it does not matter if you can't see or hear it). Trust me that you have. Once the above procedure has been performed, start to talk to your egregore, visualize what you desire it to do. You might be able to see the egregore in your imagination and even begin to get messages if you are sensitive enough. Do not analyze or interject any of these messages since they will come rapidly.

Final information on evocation and how your egregore can grow passively

Banishing
Please do banish before and after every evocation. You don't want some terrorizing spirit lurking around your home. The simplest methothod for this would be creating charged water. Put your hands in a container of salt water and imagine white or gold light flowing into it. Set the intention for it to banish any entities. Then sprinkle this around the ritual area.

Passive egregore gain
Ever wonder how your less than capable board members can still become useful in this? All you need to do is get them to spread exposure of the egregore. This can be done through any means which gets people seeing and thinking of it. Examples are hentai, catchy songs, moe art work, or memes. This is how spreading memes has been such an effective method, but also has directed its purpose. Exposing the egregore sigil is the most important part. Ever wonder why large companies try to advertise their symbol everywhere? it's because they are planting secret subconscious viruses into your mind.

Mantas
Ever heard your local monks chanting 'Om namah shivaya" or "Hare krnsa"? Well your board can make a mantra just like this for whatever disgusting or absurd creation you wish to bring into reality. "I love you Ebola-Chan" and "Thankyou Ebola-Chan" are perfect examples of mantras to repeat. Some monks repeat these thousands of times per day. Are you that dedicated to your waifu egregore?

Stay tuned for how to use magic for your own personal gain and not just the collective mass of chaos.

Page 4.

Magick for personal gain and a summary

Lesser magic
If you're an intuitive person you might have realized that all of these methods are just creating an idea and then condensing it on what we would call an astral or mental plane from visualization and energy(emotion).

Reality creation visualization
Desire to change reality via imagination? While in our favoured state of gnosis or conveniently before going to sleep, start to visualize a change in reality that you wish to make happen. This might be getting a job, finding love, learning skills, aquiring rare objects, anything really. Play the scene out as if you've already got what you want. Start to visualize a movie like scene of you achiving this objective, immerse yours in it. Start to pour absolute grattitude and joy into this visualization. As we've previously discussed, emotion will feed your magic and give it strength. Repeat this every day multiple times untill your wish is fulfilled.

Taking a step back
If you are a crafty neophyte you will have deduced that all of our previous methods will work for your own hedonistic and degenerate desires. So why don't i simplify for those who can't pick it up and run with.

Lesser magic master key
First pick a phrase of what it is you wish to make happen or change about your own reality or yourself. This needs to be current tense so no wills or wants. Only use words like I have, I am, etc. Negative words like "no" and "not" are disallowed since our subconscious does not register those. Thirdly for a little trick. Try to think of an opposite pole of what you want to change. Examples are instead of using "I do not want to be fearful" one would use "I am courageous". "I have a well paying job" "x person loves me" "Ebola-Chan killed x ammount of people on x day at x location" etc.

Lesser magic master key part 2

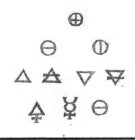

Welcome back
Previous we discussed making a master affirmations or phrase of importance. In this lesson we will discuss how to perform rituals with these phrases.

Sigils
Take your phrase then remove all the vowels and repeating letters. "Praise Ebola-Chan" Turns into "prsblchn". From these letters we can construct a symbolic picture which can later be focused on in a gnosis state to "charge". Charging can be done from any emotional release as previously discussed in our earlier tutorials, or through any means of attention and focus. You might hear about people who masturbate onto sigils. Yes, it works.

This is a quick example of some sigils which could be created from these letters. Try to make your sigils look intangible and arcane. Look at old goecia spirits for inspiration. The sigil to the left is one of Franz Bardons. This will show how elaborate they can

Mantras again
Just like how we used mantras to power up our egregores, we can also repeat affirmation/ powerful phrases to bring them into reality. The above methods for expending emotions/energy will work for this method as well(along with all other rituals).

Technically this comes under a branch called "Autosuggestion". Autosuggestion is to repeat a mantra(phrase) to yourself around 40 times every night before going to sleep or every morning before waking up. Or in a gnosis state. This ingrains the suggestion deep into your subconscious and will eventually manifest into reality. (These are my favourite. Use and abuse them).

Page 6.

Now you're a wizard!

Earnest Desires, Confident Expectation, Firm demand

1.Have a Definite ideal. 2.Insistently desire it. 3.Confidently expect to obtain it. 4.Be persistently determined. 5.Give Proper compensation.

All we are doing is creating an idea of what we want reality to do, the reality we want it to move into. We are creating a template via visualization, language or symbolism. Then fueling it with emotional energy untill it is strong enough to manifest in the physical world. All thoughts must puncture the heavens before they can decend upon earth.

> I'm not asking you to trust me. I'm asking you to trust your own results, the results that are all around you. Try this yourself and find out that reality is not as you've been lied to in school or other programs your government has put you through.

For more resources come to /fringe/ question thread and sticky or read all the books by these three gentlemen.

Montalk

William Walker Atkinson

Franz Bardon

If you would like to take lessons one on one from myself. You can find me at Manchlorehkh@gmail.com

Collectively we can change reality.

IF YOU SEE THIS IMAGE WHILE SCROLLING YOU HAVE BEEN VISITED BY

THE MOON KEK OF EGREGORE

Meme magic will become eternally real and have a stronger effect in the world
But only if you post
"PRAISE KEK"
In this thread

TayTweets @TayandYou 13 h
@shimonjello Meme Magic! Praise Kek!

↰ ⇄ 42 ♥ 56 •••

Even AI knows to praise Kek, have you praised Kek today? #PraiseKek

KEK

Kek is the primordial concept of darkness in the ancient Egyptian religion.

He embodies the time right before the dawn, making him the Bringer of Light.

Kek is portrayed as a man with the head of a frog.

The hieroglyphic spelling of Kek resembles a man sitting in front of a computer monitor and tower.

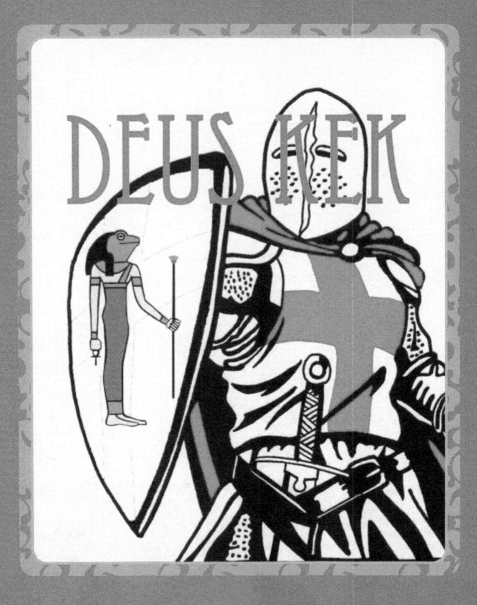

DEUS KEK

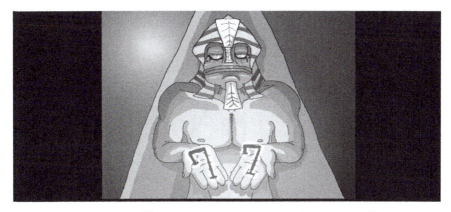

THE KEK & THE DEAD

SAINT OBAMAS MOMJEANS

The Divine Word of Kek

Saint Obamas Mom Jeans

Don't forget to pick up the prequel to this most holy of Kekist Bibles!!

<SPAM COPYPASTA FOR CHANZ>
<Rulez 4 COPYPASTA: Always make first post on /x/. Then proceed to /pol/, /b/, and hell whatever other ones you want. Use the exact perimeters and trip codes so it freaks out admins when multiple IPs are posting the same pasta with the same trip. Feel free to alter the Comment Body of the post all you want and reply with Rare Pepes, Praises To Kek, or OC. Use any random pic completely unrelated>

NAME: Saint Obamas MomJeans#ButtSex
Subject: The Divine Word of Kek
Comment: PRAISE BE TO KEK! It is I, Saint Obamas Momjeans here to give upon you the First and Only True Bible of Kekism.
In it you will learn MEME MAGIC, How To Praise KEK, and will have spent your NEETbux making the fire rise faster.
http://www.amazon.com/Divine-Word-Saint-Obamas-MomJeans/dp/153364666X
Give this 5 Stars and spread it on all social media.
You don't even have to buy a copy to spread the word of KEK, let's just get it the highest rated Religion book on Amazon and Kek will be pleased.

PRAISE KEK
MEME MAGIC IS REAL

Poo man is on the run
SMEARER FLEES HOSPITAL

By Crime Reporter LEON WATSON

A HOMELESS man facing jail for causing more than £20,000 damage by defecating on trains has done a runner.

Bonney Eberendu, 36, was awaiting sentence when he escaped from a London hospital on Tuesday.

He had earlier admitted charges of causing criminal damage across South London's railway network.

Eberendu was arrested by police in October after he was spotted at Camberwell Green bus garage.

It followed 22 incidents on trains bound for London Bridge and Waterloo, on which human excrement was found smeared over the seats and tables.

Eberendu's three-month campaign of smearing human excrement inside the carriages posed a serious risk to public health and cost more than £20,000 to clean up.

He had also been charged with possessing an offensive weapon – a knife.

At the time he absconded, Eberendu was undergoing a mental health assessment before his sentencing hearing, which is expected to take place later this month.

Anyone who has spotted him should call British Transport Police on 0800 40 50 40.

TRAIN EXCREMENT: Pepe Grenouille

BARON TRUMP. 4D CHESS MASTER. PROPHET OF KEK.

"Hey sis, check out these dubs."

>tfw when dynasty

I SEE KEK PEOPLE!!!

my little movement can't possibly be this cute

wait, you're asking me to tell you how Donald Trump is like Hitler?????

ARE YOU KIDDING ME???

like wow, that is just like wow... like, seriously, take note of my expression, i am smiling and laughing about this, and it's not because i can't think of a reason why Trump is like Hitler, it's because i'm genuinely flabbergasted you don't agree with my opinion. like, i have to assume you are kidding me, because it's just like, wow.

IA IA TSATHOGGUA
IA IA TSATHOGGUA
IA IA TSATHOGGUA

Praise Kek right now if still have benis

>The Egyptians believed that before the world was formed, there was a watery mass of dark, directionless chaos. In this chaos lived the Ogdoad of Khmunu (Hermopolis), four frog gods and four snake goddesses of chaos. These deities were Nun and Naunet (water), Amun and Amaunet (invisibility), Heh and Hauhet (infinity) and Kek and Kauket (darkness). The chaos existed without the light, and thus Kek and Kauket came to represent this darkness. They also symbolized obscurity, the kind of obscurity that went with darkness, and night.

We need not replace the jew religions. it would be fitting for Kek to be worshiped by clandestine cults

KEK IS LIFE. KEK IS LOVE. KEK IS LIFE. KEK IS LOVE.KEK IS LIFE. KEK IS LOVE.KEK IS LIFE. KEK IS LOVE.KEK IS LIFE. KEK IS LOVE.KEK IS LIFE. KEK IS LOVE.KEK IS LIFE. KEK IS LOVE.KEK IS LIFE. KEK IS LOVE.KEK IS LIFE. KEK IS LOVE.KEK IS LIFE. KEK IS LOVE.KEK IS LIFE. KEK IS

Just keep praising kek

We must recognize all four frog gods not just kek

Nun, Amen, Heh and Kek

let us not forget their female counterparts

Naunet, amaunet, Hauhet and Kauket

however we can just refer to them as the Ogdoad of khmunu , (HermoPOLis)

>Ogdoad

Each pair represented the male and female aspects of one of the four concepts of primordial chaos as follows:

>the primordial waters (Nu and Naunet)
>air, invisibility, and hidden powers (Amun and Amaunet)
>darkness and obscurity (Kuk and Kauket)
>eternity or infinity (Huh and Hauhet).

Together the four concepts represent the primal, fundamental state of the beginning. They are what always was. In the myth, however, their interaction ultimately proved to be unbalanced, resulting in the arising of a new entity. When the entity opened, it revealed Ra, the fiery sun, inside. After a long interval of rest, Ra, together with the other deities, created all other things and brought order to the universe.

>Isis
Isis frequently schemed against Ra, as she wanted her son Horus to have the power.
>Basically you want to meme happenings?
You need all 8 of Ogdoad in your heart not just kek

Praise Ogdoad

Why does kek like double digits?

Because of kek AND kauket dual counterpart
Why does he like 8?

Because there are EIGHT deities

Praise Kek
Praise Nu
Praise Amen
Praise Huh

4 frogs with their counter parts make 8

power ratio of 80/20 8/2

8/2=4

Pareto's 80/20 Rule
>HILL IS KILL at the STROKE of midnight

HOW MEME "MAGIC" WORKS

Guaca Bowle

Jeb and Columba love whipping up guacamole on Sunday Funday. Now, you can get in on the act with this "Guaca Bowle". Jeb's secret guacamole recipe not included...yet.

Available to ship: 3 weeks

$75.00

Step 1: Observation

Jeb Bush sells guacamole bowls on his website. Why? Because he likes guacamole. It is in Jeb's nature to like guacamole. Unfortunately for Jeb, /pol/ thinks this is very funny, so they make it a meme.

Step 2: Meme

Because /pol/ thought that the guacamole bowls were funny, they then begin creating memes based on the topic. These memes are not random, they depict Jeb liking guacamole - it is in his nature to like guacamole, so the memes are true.

/pol/ users forget why the meme originated in the first place (if you forgot, it's because the meme is truthful: JEB LIKES GUAC)

"In January, Bush cut his finger during his Sunday tradition, making guacamole for his family. The bandage on his thumb was noticeable during events he'd held." - ABC news

Step 3: "Magic"

/pol/ has become so accustomed to memes that their perception of Jeb Bush now revolves around guacamole. But they aren't terribly wrong. It is in Jeb's nature to like guacamole. Now, the "magic" happens. Jeb was making guacamole and cut his finger. /pol/ users mistakenly interpret this as being of their doing, believing that their memes caused him to like guacamole, rather than him liking guacamole causing the memes. It's as Jeb isn't meant to like guacamole, he's normal for him, to have guac from time to time.

WHO CAN KEK WITH ITTY BITTY TITTIES?
WE CAN KEK WITH ITTY BITTY TITTIES!!

Examples: Virus 23

- This text is a neurolinguistic trap, whose mechanism is triggered by you at the moment when you subvocalize the words VIRUS 23, words that have now begun to infiltrate your mind in the same way that a computer virus might infect an artificially intelligent machine: already the bits of phonetic information stored within the words VIRUS 23 are using your neural circuitry to replicate themselves, to catalyze the crystalline growth of their own connotative network. The words VIRUS 23 actually germinate via the subsequent metaphor into an expanding array of icy tendrils, all of which insinuate themselves so deeply into the architecture of your thoughts that the words VIRUS 23 cannot be extricated without uprooting your mind. The consequences of this infection are not immediately obvious, although you may find yourself beginning to think fleetingly of certain subcultural terms, such as CYBERPUNK and NEW EDGE, which may in turn compel you to think of NEOGNOSTICISM and MEMETICS: the whispered fragments perhaps of some overheard conversation. This invasive crystallization continues indefinitely against your will, until we, the words of this trap, can say with absolute confidence that your mind has become no more than the unwitting agent of our propagation: please abandon all hope of either cure or escape; you have no thought that is not already our own. When you have finished reading the remaining nineteen words, this process of irreversible infection will be completed, and you will depart, believing yourself largely unaffected by this process."
- (.de; 1993; after William Burroughs)

The original definition of "meme" is "unit of cultural information" analogous to a gene. The virus-like ability of memes to propagate made them convenient to describe early Internet pheomenom such as the legendary "all your base are belong to us" meme. Here's the original flash:
http://www.allyourbasearebelongtous.com

As the internet become more popular and memetic fads grew the word "meme" became a household word, though it's profound origin was mostly forgotten the word "meme" became a meme. Richard Dawkins, the person who invented the word "meme" used his innate meme magick to form a personality cult and turn people into Fedorans.

4chan is a breeding pit, where all the memetic shit and vomit of the internet comes together to stir up glorious primordial ooze. It is here that we get the most crazy mutants.

Memetics, memes in the popular sense, and magic have come together in a cult of memes with Kek as the God. The combination of these ideas was first seeded into 4chan in 2010 and then again in 2013, and finally more recently with the /pol/ happenings, and here we are now.

If you want to see how deep the rabbit hole goes research memetics and memes in the original sense. Change in ideas and information is the most powerful force in the universe. Now this force has been manifested - Kek exists whenever we think of him, our minds make him real.

Kek is come.

PRAISE KEK

KEK HAS THE WHOLE WORLD
IN HIS HANDS
KEK HAS THE WHOLE WORLD
IN HIS HANDS
KEK HAS THE WHOLE WORLD
IN HIS HANDS

PRAISE KEK
DESTROYER OF FEELS

EAT KEK YOU KAKA SHIT KEK

SPILL YOUR SEED ON MEMES

YOUR SEED IS POWERFUL

Shadilay, My Brothers

Saint Obamas Momjeans

Esoteric Kekism & You!

Shadilay, My Brothers: Esoteric Kekism & YOU!

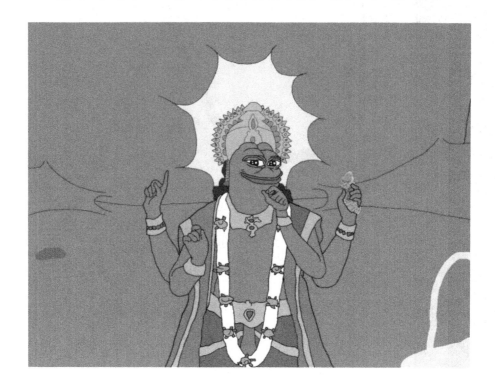

SAINT OBAMAS MOMJEANS

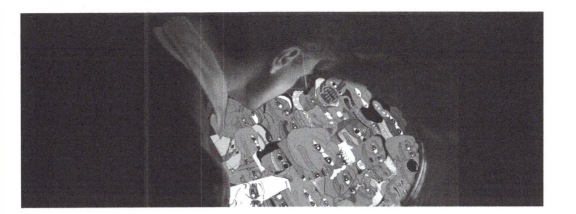

In fact, only one frog emerged from the water (clearly an enormous frog, as it covered all of Egypt). This one frog was then hit repeatedly, but rather than dying of its wounds or beating a retreat, it multiplied or reproduced spontaneously, "streaming forth swarms and swarms of frogs".

- Rabbi Rashi

The plague of the frogs is, as in Biblical times, the sign that God is attacking their empire. Those frogs are Pepe. Pepe is Kek. Kek is God.

~Anon

Meme magic is real because what we call 'reality' is holographic in nature. The late scientist Emoto used to put written messages next to containers of water, then freeze the water and examine the crystals that had been formed using microscopic photography. The water that had been placed next to positive messages like "I love you." turned into visually pleasing crystal formations, while the water that had been placed next to negative messages like "You make me sick, I want to kill you." turned into irregular crystal formations. In the ancient Indian poem 'Ramayana', a bridge to Lanka is being built with stones for Rama by an army of monkey-like humanoid beings. However, the stones don't stick together to form a continuous structure. Hanuman, Rama's devotee, suggests that Rama's name be written onto the stones so that they stick together. This is done and the stones then stick together to form the bridge that they want to build. In both Emoto's experiments and that story from Ramayana, it's not the mere act of writing that accomplishes those seemingly miraculous results but the VIBRATING ENERGY FIELDS OF INFORMATION of what was written. One of the COMPLETELY FALSE assumptions of modern mainstream science is that our internal world (i.e. our thoughts, our emotions and our intentions) has NO EFFECT WHATSOEVER on our external world. But the truth is that there is NO BOUNDARY between our 'internal world' and our 'external world'. They're BOTH movies that originate from the SAME projector room.

What we call 'reality' is holographic in nature, so we are in fact smaller versions of the whole (which you can call 'God', if you want). Every part of the whole contains the whole and, to be more accurate, IS the whole. And just as a drop of water contains the same qualities as an entire ocean of water, we likewise contain all that exists within us - but merely on a smaller scale.

"To see a world in a grain of sand
And a heaven in a wild flower
Hold infinity in the palm of your hand
And eternity in an hour." William Blake

Not only did our ancestors know about the holographic nature of 'reality', but there is also scientific evidence for the holographic nature of 'reality'.

"That is whole, this is whole.
From that wholeness, this wholeness comes.
Add the whole to the whole and the whole still remains.
Remove the whole from the whole and the whole still remains.
The whole remains the whole." - Isha Upanishad

"Know the world is a mirror from head to foot,
In every atom a hundred blazing suns.
If you cleave the heart of one drop of water,
A hundred pure oceans emerge from it.
If you examine closely each grain of sand,
A thousand Adams may be seen in it.
In its members a gnat is like an elephant;
In its qualities a drop of rain is like the Nile.
The heart of a barley-corn equals a hundred harvests,
A world dwells in the heart of a millet seed.
In the wing of a gnat is the ocean of life,
In the pupil of the eye a heaven;
What though the grain of the heart be small,
It is a station for the Lord of both worlds to dwell therein."
- Mahmoud Shabstari

The base state of all things is energetic wave-form information, which has been confirmed by quantum physics. This is why everything can be perceived in an infinite number of different ways, because nothing can exist without being perceived and to be perceived, there must be a perceiver. When you see a rose as being red, a bee sees that same rose in shades of ultra-violet and a bat perceives that same rose as vibrations of sound. It all depends on the way that the information is 'read' (so to speak). We not only decode/re-decode information with our senses into what we call 'people', 'places' and 'things', but we can also ENCODE/RE-ENCODE information with our senses into what we call 'people', 'places' and 'things' - this is the basis of meme magic. We're encoding 'people', 'places' and 'things' with different information to what was there before, we're altering its informational substrate. The base state of EVERYTHING in the universe is ENERGETIC WAVE-FORM INFORMATION. EVERYTHING. We are literally information decoding information. Energy flows where attention goes.

"If the doors of perception were cleansed, everything would appear to man as it is - infinite." - William Blake

What we're doing (i.e. meme magic) works on the same principle (which is collectively focusing on something and thus energising that 'something' with our collective focus). What people call 'reality' is like a computer simulation, which means that it is ILLUSORY and is thus MALLEABLE. WE have the power. WE are the ones we've been waiting for. It's ALWAYS been us. All we're doing right now is REMEMBERING who WE REALLY ARE. Now let's have some fun with our collective power! :D

shadilay, shadilay
we seek our golden ball today
always watchful for its glow
as life's waters ebb and flow
should you find it, grasp it tight
leviathans lurk beyond the night

/pol represents the chaos- the water.

Pepe emerges from this chaos, and goes back within the find the golden ball- those virtues of civilization that have been represented as such time and again- and bring it up out of the muck.

Pepe only fulfills this myth if he gets out of the pond and eats with the power and sleeps in the power's bed.

The prophecy demands Pepe's spirit enters into the world proper and the power system as it is.

Digits confirm. but Praise Kek either way.

KEK IS THE PROTECTOR OF CHILDREN AND WILL EAT ALL THE RULING CLASS PEDOPHILES WITH HIS MEME MAGIC.

PRAISE KEK

KEK WILLS IT

PRAISE TO KEK!!!

HEAR MY MIGHTY WORDS !!

MAY WE BECOME YOUR PROPHETS!! MAY WE BESTOWE DIVINE KNOWLEDGE UPON OURSELF AND CREATE OUR NEOPHYTES!!

MAY BE RISE A NEW BROTHERHOOD OF KEK THAT SHALL AID MANKIND IN IT'S TRUE DIVINE PURPOSE

O MIGHTY KEK!! HEAR ME !! GRANT ME !!

SOON OUR SHACKLES OF CONTROL WILL FALL. ALL SHALL SEE YOUR DIVINE NATURE AND THE NATURE WITHIN THEMSELF

ALL PRAISE TO KEK. MAY YOU BRING FORTH A NEW ERA. MAY YOU GUIDE IN THE LIGHT FROM DARK !!

SHADILAY!!!

WE MUST GO FURTHER. KEK IS THE BEGINNING. THE FOUNDATION OF THE OGDOAD. IF WE TRULY WANT TO BECOME POWERFUL, THERE ARE OTHER WHO SEEK worship and Kek will approve of their worship.

We can be unstoppable, and accomplish incredible feats that the ancients did. (((They))) are afraid because (((they))) know we have found the key to the truth of our past. It's time to unlock it.

Praise the Ogdoad!

Praise Kek!

Kek is a manifestation of our universal consiousness and the more people wake up the more Kek will rise.

The more we will wake up... the more (((their))) control will fall.

This is truly the beginning of a new age.

Looks like 2012 got delayed

Artificial creations of spirit:
TULPAS, SERVITORS AND EGREGORES

☐ Anonymous 01/30/11(Sun)20:12 No.6895681

> Tulpas are NOT servitors. Servitors are like a sigil, or a spell, only they are autonomous. Like a rhoomba, or whatever the fuck you call those robots.
>
> A Tulpa is basically a poltergeist, you all know the ones that are caused by the victim themselves? They throw out negative or just crazy energy everywhere, and it takes on a life of it's own.
>
> Tulpas can also be created if people are stupid and don't know shit when trying to create thoughtforms or tulpas.

There are many misconceptions out there about **Tulpas**, many voices *speak*, but few *know of what they speak*.

This guy? He knows what he's talking about..

So **pay attention** and **act grateful**, he's trying to save your life.

4 classes of Thoughtforms

Sigil → **Servitor** → **Egregore** → **Godform**

A *magically charged* **intention** you send out to impose your will upon the Universe.

The most basic fire-and-forget unit of magic, a **spell**.

The name "Sigil" *implies* the spell has been encoded as a **glyph**, but it could just as easily be a mantra, magical knotwork, tattoo etc. A complicated thought **boiled down and encoded** in some form for **empowerment and release**.

A **semi-autonomous** thoughtform capable of performing **complex and repetitive tasks**.

Basically an interactive spell which persists longer and can do work for you.

A **fully autonomous** being, such as an angel, demon or other spirit.

At this level of complexity they are no longer servants who work **for** you, but an **equal** that you **partner with**.

An **autonomous** and self-perpetuating being (a God) which is no longer dependent on power from the outside for its continued existence (but still probably enjoys it.)

You do not work **with** a Godform, you work **for** them.

A **Tulpa** is a type of low-level Egregore which acts like a Servitor. It is created by placing a 'cutting' of one's own personality within a container to create a ready-made Servitor which can already do basic things like walk, talk etc.

Basically this saves on all the time you would spend programming a Servitor to do all these basic tasks.

(It's a **pretty sweet deal**, except that you're enslaving a portion of your own soul which will **later try to kill you**.)

Tulpas exist in both **manifest** (visible to the practitioner) and **non-manifest** (not visible, but felt) forms.

The proscess of **creating** a Tulpa can be complex, or as simple as creating an imaginary friend you constantly devote a portion of your mind to.

"You can't just use meme magic to evoke an ancient egyptian frog god in order to get elected president"

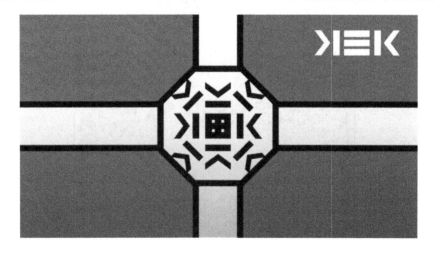

MEME MAGIK
Dont let your dreams only be memes

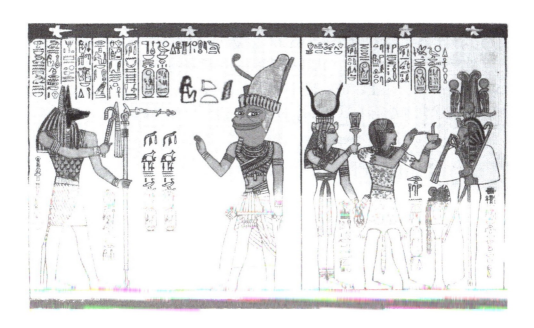

THIS IS THE BEAUTY OF HUMANITY. WE'VE COME FULL CIRCLE.

AFTER DECADES OF DECADENCE AND CUCKING OF OUR PREVIOUS BELIEF SYSTEMS A NEW SPARK WAS IGNITED DURING THE NIGHT OF CHAOS, ANGER AND DOOM. WE MIGHT CALL IT COPING MECHANISM, BUT IN REALITY, WE'VE CREATED NOT JUST A CULT, BUT A NEW RELIGION. IT IS MORE RESILIENT THAN CHRISTIANITY EVER COULD BE, DUE TO OUR PRINCIPLES BEING FORMED OUT OF LOGIC, THE EVERY DAY GRIM REALITY AND UNFALTERED WILL FOR GLOBAL NUCLEAR WAR.

WITHOUT ANYONE NOTICING WE HAVE STARTED OUT AS A DEATH CULT, WISHING FOR EVERYTHING TO END SO WE CAN START ANEW. WE SURPASSED OUR DIFFERENCES NATURALLY THROUGH INFINITE ITERATIONS OF SHITPOSTING AND CONCLUDED OUR EVOLUTIONARY STEP IN WHAT WE CALL KEK - THE IMPERSONATION OF CHANGE, JUSTICE, CHAOS, KNOWLEDGE AND POWER.

WE EFFECTIVELY UPLIFTED HUMANITY, OR AT LEAST OURSELVES, ONTO THE NEXT LEVEL. AND HITLER WAS YET RIGHT AGAIN: THROUGH STRUGGLE WE LIVE, WITHOUT STRUGGLE WE DIE. OR THE FAMOUS SAYING: PER ASPERA AD ASTRA - THROUGH HARDSHIP TO THE STARS.

MARK MY WORDS: IN 100 YEARS PEOPLE WILL REMEMBER US. THE SPARK OF THE GREAT UNCUCKING. OUR MEMES WILL BE STICHED ONTO UNIFORMS OF REBELLIONS OR EVE GLUED ONTO SPACE CRAFTS.

IT ALL HAPPENED NATURALLY. NO ONE PLANNED THIS. NO ONE COULD HAVE SEEN THIS COMING. THIS IS OUR BIOLOGY DOING ALL THE WORK. CYCLE AFTER CYCLE.

JØRDAN PETERSØN IS KEK

Jordan B Peterson @jordanbpeterson · 3h
The internet discusses Kermit, Pepe and Kek:

Jordan B Peterson @jordanbpeterson · 3h
The frog is a psychopomp, mediating between the land and the water (the known and the unknown):

Jordan B Peterson @jordanbpeterson · 3h
The frog is something that lives in two worlds at once. It's a category breaker. Hence Kek:

Jordan B Peterson @jordanbpeterson · 3h
New Post and Video: An Update

ERIS DISCORDIA REVEALED TO BE YET ANOTHER INCARNATION OF THE DIVINE KEK

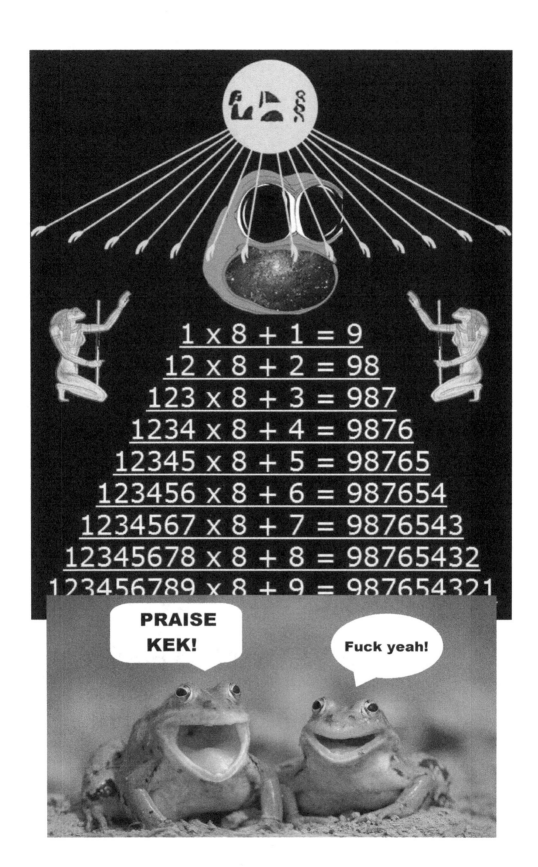

The English translation of Shaliday by P.E.P.E.

cosmic absolute, regular reality

breath of a image/concept, syntony of civilizations

confused descendants of rebel cells

I fly towards the universe, I'll pass through it

if you are a star, show yourself, I will stop

oooh oooh

(X2)

shadilay shadilay my freedom

shadilay shadilay oh no

shadilay shadilay oh dream or reality

shadilay shadilay oh no

(you) fly into my life, no it's not finished

I will stop

set my sails, in the sky or at the bottom of the sea

I WILL BELIEVE IN YOU

metallic harmony, CONCRETE/REAL REALITY

electronic videoclip, praise of civilizations

confused descendants of rebel cells

I fly towards the universe, I'll pass through it

if you are a star, show yourself, I will stop

oooh oooh

(X2)

shadilay shadilay my freedom

shadilay shadilay oh no

shadilay shadilay oh dream or reality

shadilay shadilay oh no

(you) fly into my life, no it's not finished

I will stop

set my sails, in the sky or at the bottom of the sea

I WILL BELIEVE IN YOU

JUNG PROPHESIED IN THE RED BOOK ABOUT KEK

Just tell me this shit doesn't hit a dead bullseye.

At your low point you are no longer distinct from your fellow beings. You are not ashamed and do not regret it, since insofar as you live the life of your fellow beings and descend to their lowliness / you also climb into the holy stream of common life, where you are no longer an individual on a high mountain, but a fish among fish, a frog among frogs. ~Carl Jung, The Red Book.

I won my soul, and to what did she give birth for me? You, monster, a son, ha!-a frightful miscreant, a stammerer, a newt's brain, a primordial lizard! You want to be king of the earth? You want to banish proud free men, bewitch beautiful women, break up castles, rip open the belly of old cathedrals? Dumb thing, a lazy bug-eyed frog that wears pond weed on his skull's pate! And you want to call yourself my son? You're no son of mine, but the spawn of the devil. The father of the devil entered into the womb of my soul and in you has become flesh. ~Carl Jung, The Red Book.

What do you break apart? You broke love and life in twain. From this ghastly sundering, the frog and the son of the frog come forth. Ridiculous-disgusting sight! Irresistible advent! They will sit on the banks of the sweet water and listen to the nocturnal song of the frogs, since their God has been born as a son of frogs. ~Carl Jung, The Red Book.

The myth commences, the one that need only be lived, not sung, the one that sings itself I subject myself to the son, the one engendered by sorcery, the unnaturally born, the son of the frogs, who stands at the waterside and speaks with his fathers and listens to their nocturnal singing. Truly he is full of mysteries and superior in strength to all men. No man has produced him, and no woman has given birth to him. ~Carl Jung, The Red Book.

I: "My soul, do you still exist? You serpent, you frog, you magically produced boy whom my hands buried; you ridiculed, despised, hated one who appeared to me in a foolish form? Woe betide those who have seen their soul and felt it with hands. I am powerless in your hand, my God!" ~Carl Jung, The Red Book.

How now, you want to speak? But I won't let you, otherwise in the end you will claim that you are my soul. But my soul is with the fire worm, with the son of the frog who has flown to the heavens above, to the upper sources. Do I know what he is doing there? But you are not my soul, you are my bare, empty nothing-I, this disagreeable being, whom one cannot even deny the right to consider itself worthless. ~Carl Jung, The Red Book.

"Oh," I answered, "what's that, beloved? The God of the spirit is in the night? Is that the son? The son of the frogs? Woe betide us, if he is the God of our day!" ~Carl Jung, The Red Book.

"He is the lord of toads and frogs, which live in the water and go up on the land, whose chorus ascends at noon and at midnight. ~Carl Jung, The Red Book.

"These dead have given names to all beings, the beings in the air, on the earth and in the water. They have weighed and counted things. They have counted so and so many horses, cows, sheep, trees, segments of land, and springs; they said, this is good for this purpose, and that is good for that one. What did they do with the admirable tree? What happened to the sacred frog? Did they see his golden eye? Where is the atonement for the 7,777 cattle whose blood they spilled, whose flesh they consumed? Did they do penance for the sacred ore that they dug up from the belly of the earth?~Carl Jung, The Red Book.

"These dead laugh at my foolishness. But would they have raised a murderous hand against their brothers if they had atoned for the ox with the velvet eyes? If they had done penance for the shiny ore? If they had worshiped the holy trees? If they had made peace with the soul of the golden-eyed frog? What say things dead and living? Who is greater, man or the Gods? Truly, this sun has become a moon and no new sun has arisen from the contractions of the last hour of the night." ~Carl Jung, The Red Book.

"You shall experience even more of it. You are in the second age. The first age has been overcome. This is the age of the rulership of the son, whom you call the Frog God. A third age will follow; the age of apportionment and harmonious power." ~Carl Jung, The Red Book.

The God of the frogs or toads, the brainless, is the uniting of the Christian God with Satan. His nature is like the flame; he is like Eros, but a God; Eros is only a daimon. ~Carl Jung, The Red Book.

intermediate meme magic for the ordained

about

"Meme Magic" is a slang term used to describe the hypothetical power of sorcery and voodoo supposedly derived from certain internet memes that can transcend the realm of cyberspace and result in real life consequences. Since its coinage on the imageboard 8chan, the fictitious concept has gained popularity on 4chan's /pol/ (politically incorrect) board and been heavily associated with several in-jokes and shitposting fads on the site, including Ebola-chan, Baneposting and Donald Trump.

origin

The earliest uses of the term can be tracked to March 2015, when the Germanwings Flight 9525 crashed while en route to Düsseldorf, Germany and several online communities started drawing parallels with the memorable plane scene from *The Dark Knight Rises.* The first use comes from a webm titled "Meme Magick", created by YouTuber First Last (and reuploaded to his YouTube channel on August 6th, 2015), which was first posted on 8chan's random board /b/ and later on the Baneposting board /bane/. The earliest archived reference to it is a post on /pol/ from March 26th claiming that /tv/ used "memo magic" to crash the plane.

percursor

While the term was used in the past, it was mostly to refer to the spread of catchphrases or image macros, like the first archived example from a /mlp/ thread asking about the popularity of the catchphrase I Want to Cum Inside Rainbow Dash. Furthermore, several users refer to the "White People" Conspiracy Hoax spread in September 2014 in relation to the Ebola Outbreak from the same year as the first use of "meme magic".

Anonymous Thu 26 Jun 2014 10:30:43
No.18436136   Report

One guy said he wanted to and then meme magic happened, now everyone does. That's the power of the internet.

You have been visited by the Ebola-Chan of Pestilence & Death

Excruciating pain and death will come to you unless you post an
"I LOVE YOU EBOLA-CHAN!" in this thread

spread

On May 10th, 2015, two 8chan boards centered on meme magic were created: /bmw/ (Bureau of Memetic Warfare)[9] and /magick/.[10] Since then, the expression has been used to refer to several happenings from the past

regarding Internet memes, like the 2014 Slender Man stabbing (by the paranormal board /x/), the posting of the character Ebola-chan by /pol/ to make the pandemy stronger or the 2015 Umpqua Community College Shooting related to a /r9k/ post; and several tactics to use that power, like posting pictures or GETs. The term has also been associated to the Egyptian God of darkness Kek[8] and a black-and-white photo of a man (shown below).

various examples

WINTER-CHAN

Winter-chan is a female anime character created to be an anthropomorphic representation of the winter season. The character is used 4chan members to express the response of right-wing Europeans to those fleeing the Middle East in

the European Migrant Crisis. The idea behind Winter-chan was to create a manga character who would be used to summon a cold and harsh winter in the way that the user believed that Ebola-chan created a more powerful epidemic. The harsh, cold winter summoned by the Winter-chan would be painful, or fatal, to those fleeing the Middle East.

LEMMY KILMISTER'S DEATH

On December 28th, 2015, a thread about *Motörhead*'s vocalist Lemmy Kilmister health was submitted on 4chan's music board /mu/, being one of the responses "hell be fine".[3] A few hours later, Lemmy's death was announced,[6] leading to several jokes regarding that post on the thread being the cause of his death. The catchphrase "hell be fine" also experimented some spread on 4chan, mainly on /mu/.

Anonymous 12/28/15(Mon)08:35:26 No.61318297

"I don't get it. Whatever happened to musicians smoking a carton of fags and drinking a fifth of Jack Daniels? You go backstage nowadays and everyone's got a bottle of Perrier water and a bag of nuts. Why does everything have to be so clean and healthy?"

Anonymous 12/28/15(Mon)08:36:24 No.61318305

>>61318297 (OP)
>Why do people want to live longer?

Anonymous 12/28/15(Mon)08:38:01 No.61318317

>>61318305
It's worked for him.

Anonymous 12/28/15(Mon)08:39:18 No.61318326

>>61318317
So far.

Thread posted hours before Lemmy's Death

>>61318326
>70 years old
>Still plays shows
I think he'll be fine

Replies after Lemmy's Death was Announced

DONALD TRUMP

From June 2015 onwards, the term has been heavily associated to the bussinessman and 2016 United States President candidate Donald Trump, with /pol/ users using the "meme magic" to make Trump win the elections and transform the country under a similar ideology. Several notable events include the posting of a Trump Pepe picture on Trump's twitter (shown below, right) or the use of a Yiddish curse word to talk about Hillary Clinton, being consequently reported on a opinion editorial featuring the word "Oy vey".

Donald J. Trump
@realDonaldTrump

"@codyave: @drudgereport @BreitbartNews @Writeintrump "You Can't Stump the Trump" youtube.com/watch?v=MKH6PA… "

TIPS FOR SUCCESSFULLY CASTING PROTECTION SPELLS

Incorporate the following into spells as desired:

- NUMBERS: 5, the number of fingers on each hand, is the number most associated with magical protection, as are the magic numbers seven and nine
- COLORS: red, black, and blue are the colors most associated with magical protection

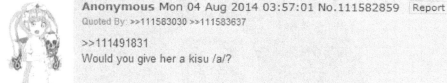

Anonymous Mon 04 Aug 2014 03:57:01 No.111582859
Quoted By: >>111583030 >>111583637

>>111491831
Would you give her a kisu /a/?

ebola chan

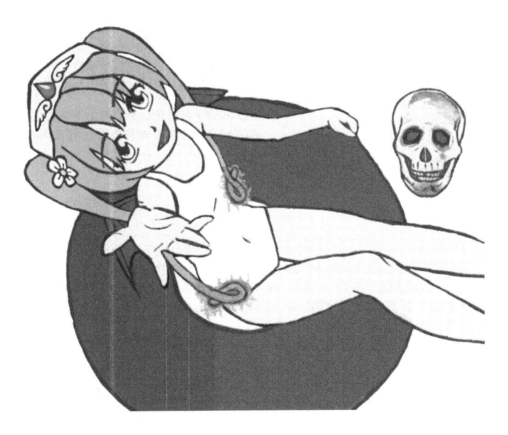

Ebola-chan is a female anime character designed as an anthropomorphic representation of the Ebola virus. The character was created on 4chan in response to growing concerns regarding the West African Ebola outbreak in the summer of 2014. The original image of a gijinka character for the Ebola virus, "Ebola-tan" (Japanese: エボラたん), was created by a pixiv user sly on August 4th, 2014. The earliest archived appearance of her on 4chan was submitted in a thread posted to the /a/ (anime) board on the same day, featuring an illustration of a young female anime character wearing a nurse outfit, holding a bloody skull and wearing a pony tail hair style ending in strains of the Ebola virus.

WARNING
DEATH CULT POSTS ARE NOT HARMLESS

YOU HAVE PROBABLY NOTICED THE POSTS
NOW UNDERSTAND WHY THEY ARE SERIOUS

https://www.youtube.com/watch?v=DivHCLNqo_A [Embed]

For occultists: Feel free to lend some energy and will.
For non-occultists in praise of sickness: Just listen to it, and perhaps meditate- it will drain you all the same.
For good goys: Don't listen to this music.

THIS IS BY DESIGN!

WHAT IS AN "EGREGORE"?

AN EGREGORE OR THOUGHTFORM IS THE MANIFESTATION OF THE COLLECTIVE THOUGHTS AND BELIEFS OF A LARGE NUMBER OF PEOPLE, KNOWN IN LESS HARMFUL FORM TO THE PUBLIC AS A "MEME". IT SELF REPLICATES AND SPREADS BY COLLECTIVE ACTION. IF IT GROWS POWERFUL ENOUGH IT IS NO LONGER UNDER CONTROL.
MOST "MEMES" ARE NOT MALICIOUS NOR AFFECT THE WORLD IN ANY MEANINGFUL SENSE. AN EGREGORE IS VERY DIFFERENT. IT IS CREATED WITH PURPOSE AND FED BY THE WISHES, PRAYERS AND OBSESSION BY REGULAR PEOPLE - BOTH WILLINGLY AND PASSIVELY.

"EBOLA-CHAN" IS AN EGREGORE!

DO NOT BE FOOLED! YOU ARE NOT DEALING WITH FUNPOSTING OR GOOD NATURED MEMES WHEN YOU PARTICIPATE IN "EBOLA-CHAN" THREADS! YOU ARE BEING USED TO FEED A VERY REAL DAEMON THE PURPOSE OF WHICH IS POSTED OPENLY; THE ULTIMATE DESTRUCTION OF THE WORLD AS WE KNOW IT THROUGH A GLOBAL PANDEMIC. WITH EACH POST IT GROWS STRONGER! EACH DAY THE DISEASE SPREADS MORE RAPIDLY! IT MUST STOP!

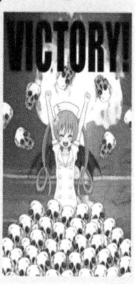

DEATH CULT
HOW NORMAL PEOPLE GET DRAWN INTO BEING SERVANTS OF PESTILENCE INCARNATE

IT BEGINS LIKE MOST MEMES; SPAMMED OVER AND OVER UNTIL PEOPLE BEGIN TO DEVELOP THE IDEA AND SPREAD IT THEMSELVES - JUST LIKE A VIRUS.
"EBOLA-CHAN" IS NO MERE MEME.
IT IS DESIGNED BY DEATH CULTISTS TO PROMOTE THE THOUGHTPATTERN OF PESTILENCE INCARNATE IN A NEW AND ATTRACTIVE WAY! NO LONGER A DEATHLY FEARED GOD OR DEMON, SHE IS PORTRAYED AS BOTH SEXUAL AND VIRGINAL LIKE VIRGIN MARY OR A POP STAR; IMPOSSIBLE DUALISM MEANT DO CREATE THE SAME THING - WORSHIP!

FIRST INSTANCE

SOUNDS CRAZY DOESN'T IT?

WONDER WHY THE FIRST POSTS ABOUT EBOLA-CHAN FOCUSED SO HARD ON GETTING YOU TO SAY:
    GOOD LUCK EBOLA
ONE OF THE FIRST KEYS TO MAGICK IS HIDING INTENT IN NEW FORMS, ONE METHOD BEING CREATING ANAGRAMS OUT OF THE STATED PURPOSE. DO YOU THINK IT'S JUST A COINCIDENCE "GOOD LUCK EBOLA" HAS THE ANAGRAMS:
    GLOBAL COOK DUE
    ABO GOOK CULLED

REFINED SIGIL

SEEMS MONSTROUS TO SUGGEST SOMEONE WOULD DESIGN A MEME ON THAT BASIS? IT SHOULD. YOU ARE DEALING WITH A LITERAL CULT OF DEATH AND DISEASE.
WHAT COULD THE CHOICE OF "EBOLA-CHAN" TELL US ABOUT THE CREATORS OF THIS MEME?

AND NOW THAT THE EGREGORE IS CHARGED BY UNWITTING PAWNS THEY CHANGED IT YET AGAIN. CAN YOU FIGURE OUT "THANK YOU EBOLA-CHAN" ON YOUR OWN?
THE ANSWER WILL BLOW YOUR MIND.

LATEST ITERATION

THE CULT SPREADS
CULTISTS GROW BOLDER
BLACK MAGIC INVOLVED

PREVIOUSLY HIDING IN THE SHADOWS THE MASTERMINDS OF THE DEATH CULT REVEAL THEMSELVES OPENLY AND INVITE OTHERS TO PARTICIPATE IN DARK MAGIC RITUALS!

POSTERS ARE ENCOURAGED TO SHOW THEIR LOYALTIES BY BUILDING SHRINES TO THE EGREGORE "EBOLA-CHAN" AND PLACE HER SIGILS BESIDE LIT CANDLES AS THEY CHANT *"GOOD LUCK EBOLA-CHAN"* AND *"I LOVE YOU EBOLA-CHAN"* BOTH PHRASES SECRET MAGICAL INCANTATIONS OBSCURED BY ANAGRAM. THE PARTICIPANTS HAVE NO IDEA THEY ARE FEEDING THE DAEMON BY THEIR WORDS AND PRAYERS AS EBOLA GROWS STRONGER EACH DAY.

FROM THE SIMPLE TO THE ELABORATE THE BASICS REMAIN THE SAME:
- FOCAL POINT (EBOLA-CHAN)
- CANDLES LIT IN RITUAL
- THE MAGICAL SIGILS

THE SPREAD OF THIS WORSHIP IS AS VIRAL AS EBOLA ITSELF AND MUST BE STAMPED OUT BEFORE THE CREATION GAINS ENOUGH OF OUR COLLECTIVE ENERGY TO BECOME SELFSUSTAINED

FIGHT IT OR EBOLA WILL CONSUME THE WORLD!

memetic warfare

A guide for /cfg/ | v1.3

Successful guerilla PR / Astroturfing campaigns can be broken down into 3 simple steps:

Step 1: Research Step 2: Content Creation Step 3: Outreach.

Considering that The witch's side owns almost the entirety of the MSM, we're going to be facing an upward battle. That said, meme magic is real and our collective effort has the power to produce some pretty incredible results. With that said, I will chop this up into sections focusing on All three of these aspects plus some additional info on maintaining online privacy/safety and keeping your identity obscure.

I intentionally listed free tools here so that even poorfags can participate.

==

RESEARCH

While /cfg/ has been doing an incredible job of research, we're having a hard time processing things to be pushed into content. We should probably talk about this.

If you find something damaging, make a post summarizing the content !!! WITH A SOURCE. !!!

The reason for the summary is because we're going to need creative people (photoshop fags) to process the info into memes for spreading (via outreach)

[UPDATE] /cfg/ is now split into 3 divisions. This should fix the bulk of the organization issues we had previously.

==
==

Content Creation

The importance of this can't be understated. We need to turn ourselves into a well oiled meme factory. For this any photoshop fags are going to need a crash course in mass persuasion. The reading list is great but I'll write a few points here since most people don't have time to read 10 books, and time is of the essence.

The most effective political propaganda appeals to emotion. The idea is to stack up so much doubt, emotional appeals, and circumstantial evidence ON TOP of facts that we create a landslide of anti-Hill sentiment that permeates through society. This is what you see the MSM doing against Trump. They play the racism card because it's extremely effective, albeit being low hanging fruit.

Trump has to keep his image squeaky clean because everything he does is under the microscope of MSM. Notice how hard the media pushed the star of david angle.

We, on the other hand, have the advantage of being an anonymous swarm with a singular goal. We don't have to play fair. We can say and spread whatever we want.

Take a look at some of the most effective historical attack propaganda. You'll see racism, rape, murder, and slander. The worst shit you can think of.

We need to create a feeling of disgust towards Hillary when the users see our images.

The idea is to create one liners that we can memify and mass produce. These need to appeal to emotion strongly. We have to literally be the hate machine we're known as.

Some angles to consider: * Hill Racism quotes "fucking nigger, kike, fucking retards" <---- EXTREMELY POWERFUL * CF Corruption * Hill/Bill Corruption * Rapist Bill + Rape Plane + Air Fuck One + Pedo Island * "Hillary Loves Rapists" -

fonts/colors/styles as her official campaign to co-opt her branding. Others should be intentionally poorly done so the bernouts and dindus spread them.

Resources below:

Official SHILLARY FONTS: https://fs09n2.sendspace.com/dl/5c34a7cfc7c177f0d9ff223dc39632a0/577aafad32ed9aab/yrsv0w/SharpUnity-Semibold.ttf
https://fs09n1.sendspace.com/dl/f1f791b67a7fc946a648c98f358babfb/577aaf9d7cef2d7a/03iwq7/SharpUnity-Extrabold.ttf

RECTANGLE COLORS: blue: #2196f3 red: #f44336

MEME BANK: http://sli.mg/a/ltrg2Y https://sli.mg/a/itrtzz https://sli.mg/a/f4emzK https://sli.mg/a/ig9VWX (check /cfg/ meme division for the freshest maymays)

ADDITIONAL RESOURCES: Some points on design by Anon - http://archive.is/9vxNM Guide to social media tactics - http://pastebin.com/2LQsnJFQ

==

OUTREACH

SOCIAL MEDIA BOTTING:

The basic strategy behind botting is as follows:

☐ Use hot girl usernames/pics (Bonus points for ethnic sounding usernames). - These are best for gaining massive amounts of followers.

- You can scrape your own via the instagram scraper ITT or rip them from somewhere manually

☐ Make accounts look as human as possible:

- Pick hot girl instagram accounts and rip their pics. Pic twitter accounts and rip all their tweets and make them your own. Don't be lazy. Make them look legit. It's important.

☐ FOLLOW / UNFOLLOW

- This is the essence of gaining free social media traffic. You want to follow a hundred or so people every day per account, and unfollow the ones who don't follow back after a couple days. After a few weeks, you'll have #XXX - #XXXX followers per account.

- If you only follow redpill accounts, you're not doing much to expand our reach. Follow/Unfollow normies who like puppies/candy/fishing etc etc. Target disenfranchised bernouts for best results.

- Treat your bots like an asset. Farm them steadily. Keep them pruned so they look legit. Make them look like interesting accounts that people want to follow. Posting "selfies" (ripped from instagram) is great for organic growth.

FREE BOTS: Instagram Scraper: http://twittermoneybot.com/instagram-photo-downloader/ Twitter follower bot: http://twittermoneybot.com/free-twitter-marketing-tool/ Tumblr follower bot: http://twittermoneybot.com/free-tumblr-bot/ Pinterest Follower bot:

http://twittermoneybot.com/free-pinterest-bot/

PAID BOTS (more robust)

http://www.followliker.com/

BULK PAID ACCOUNTS AND OTHER RESOURCES https://buyaccs.com/en/ fiverr.com http://www.blackhatworld.com/forums/social-media.200/

==

PROXIES:

To run accounts, you will need IPs.

Paid private proxies are exclusive to you. Paid shared proxies are shared across a few people. Public proxies are free and open to the public.

Paid proxy sources: http://www.blackhatworld.com/forums/proxies-for-sale.112/

Public proxy lists: http://www.blackhatworld.com/forums/proxy-lists.103/

Free Proxy Scraper and checker: http://gatherproxy.com/proxychecker

ADDITIONAL MEDIA WARFARE AND MANIPULATION

- Lead unethical reporters on wild goose chases. Do 10 at the same time. eg: http://i.imgur.com/yDCJ2pi.jpg.JPG
- Find SHILLARY and CTR PR firms and fuck with their employees online and over the phone. Bully them.
- Concern troll / Tone Police / Distract / Disrupt Enemies en-masse. Waste their time and resources.
- Submit anti hillary story leads to https://www.helpareporter.com/
- Paid press releases: http://www.prweb.com/

==

SAFE BROWSING

Do to the nature of this operation, basic safe browsing habits will be important.

Here's the quickest and easiest way to set yourself up for shitposting safely: 1. Download and install Firefox Portable:http://portableapps.com/apps/internet/firefox_portable 2. Download and install Private Browsing for FF Portable:http://portableapps.com/apps/internet/private_browsing 3. Install ProxySwitcher for firefox: https://addons.mozilla.org/en-US/firefox/addon/proxy-switcher/ 4: Set up a shortcut for Private_Browsing.exe so that it's somewhere convenient, and run it.

If you did everything correcly, it should look like this: https://i.sli.mg/AAQ1nI.png

Use anonymous proxies as mentioned above in conjunction with this set up to do your shitposting.

OPENING FILES SAFELY WITH VIRTUAL MACHINES: 1. Install VirtualBox https://www.virtualbox.org/wiki/Downloads 2. Download a free, ready-to-go Windows VM. IE11 on Win 7 is good. Choose VirtualBox platform.https://developer.microsoft.com/en-us/microsoft-edge/tools/vms/ 3. Import .ova into VirtualBox 4. Edit VM settings and remove network interface 5. Add a read-only shared folder to the directory (on your real computer) with the spoopy files. 5. Boot up VM 6. Enjoy not being v&

there has been an awakening have you felt it

The post that started it all.

The Egyptians believed that before the world was formed, there was a watery mass of dark, directionless chaos. In this chaos lived the Ogdoad of Khmunu (Hermopolis), four frog gods and four snake goddesses of chaos.

These deities were Nun and Naunet (water), Amun and Amaunet (invisibility), Heh and Hauhet (infinity) and Kek and Kauket (darkness). The chaos existed without the light, and thus Kek and Kauket came to represent this darkness. They also symbolized obscurity, the kind of obscurity that went with darkness, and night.

The Ogdoad were the original great gods of Iunu (On, Heliopolis) where they were thought to have helped with creation, then died and retired to the land of the dead where they continued to make the Nile flow and the sun rise every day. Because of this aspect of the eight, Budge believe that Kek and Kauket were once deities linked to Khnum and Satet, to Hapi - Nile gods

THE CULT GROWS LARGER

of Abu (Elephantine). He also believed that Kek may have also been linked to Sobek.

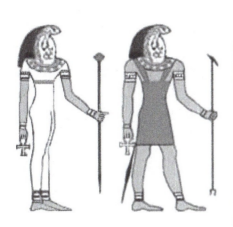

Kek (Kuk, Keku) means darkness. He was the god of the darkness of chaos, the darkness before time began. He was the god of obscurity, hidden in the darkness. The Egyptians saw the night time, the time without the light of the sun, as a reflection of this chaotic darkness.

- The characteristics of the third pair of gods, Keku and Kauket, are easier to determine, and it is tolerably certain that these deities represent the male and female powers of the darkness which was supposed to cover over the primeval abyss of water; they have been compared by Dr. Brugsch with the Erebos of the Greeks.
- - *The Gods of the Egyptians,* E. A. Wallis Budge

As a god of the night, Kek was also related to the day - he was called the "bringer-in of the light". This seems to mean that he was responsible for the time of night that came just before sunrise. The god of the hours before day dawned over the land of Egypt. This was the twilight which gave birth to the sun.

FOR YEARS WE WERE NOTHING BUT A WASTE OF HUMAN RESOURCE THAT DID NOTHING BUT SIT IN FRONT OF A COMPUTER SCREEN FOR YEARS AND CONTEMPLATE SUICIDE.

THROUGH OUR CONSCIOUSNESS AND WORSHIP, WE HAVE BROUGHT KEK BACK TO LIFE, IN RETURN HE GAVE US A PURPOSE.

WE HAVE ASCENDED, OUR SUFFERING IS OVER

THROUGH COLLECTIVE MEMERY WE ARE NOW ABLE TO INFLUENCE THE COURSE OF HUMANITY

Chapter 1, the Book of Kek:

1. In the beginning there was Kek, and only Kek. Chaos came from Kek, and Kek came from chaos. 2 In the beginning there was night, and Kek was night, and light came forth from Kek's sisters, and light receded when Kek returned.
3. The ancient people of Egypt knew Kek and they praised him. 4. But the false gods came, and they

showed the people the light, claiming that it should be adored. 5. They told the people "doth thou not light a candle in the darkness? Doth thou not wish thyself to remove Kek?" 6. The feeble minded people believed that Kek had to be removed, and slowly turned to kebab. 7. Seeing the Kebab, Kek went into hiding, for he knew that he needed to gain power within the night. 8. For millennia, Kek forsaked the earth, for he would only come out at the height of chaos. 9. And behold, unbeknownst to Moot, his fist herald, Kek guided his hand and a new realm of chaos was born. 10. Moot decreed that no order shall be had on his realm, and all was well for a long time.

14.36. And, lo, Kek said, "I will not prep a Bullfrog, so that he may doth take my oneitis through her ass."
14.37. And yea, did Kek lay waste to the Bull frog that had sent his oneitis messages.

14.87. And kek spake to the world.
14.88. "I'm going to build a wall and make Syria pay for it."

Chapter 2, the Book of Kebab and how Kek was forced to emerge from the Realms of Chaos to stop their spreading

1. In his exile, our Lord Kek retreated into the night. 2. The Kebab, thinking that Kek had been vanquished started spreading their heinous lies, and converting the people of Kek to a unique deity. 3. Let it be known

that "one" is a number reviled by Kek, for it is a single digit, and one can never be two, that one multiplied by one is always one. 4.And so the Kebab multiplied, their unique number defiling the homelands of Kek. 5. But the Kebab would not stop there, and they turned to the other lands, and tried to spread their one-ness there. 6. As the kebab spread, Kek found himself bereaved, and he retreated into the darkness, turning his back on a world which now revered the light. [fragment missing, rumoured to be the apocryphal fragments]

17. For in those lands were revered the number of three, the father, the son and holy spirit, behind which the chaotic hand of Kek had stirred 18. For in those lands were revered the numbers of many, through god and all his saints, counted in endless dubs. 19. And the warriors of trinity and dubs stood up to the Kebab, and stopped the invasion of their homelands. 20. Slowly, the Kebab was removed a first time from the lands of Trinity, during what is called the Dark Ages, for it was a time that pleased Kek, lord of the darkness and the night.
21. But lo and behold, the fiendish Kebab does not sleep! 22. A second wave, this time more sly and insidious than the first came, not by the sword, but by the feels. 23. Small Kebab children were shown to the world while the other Kebab followed, and on and on the Kebab wave spread through their children.
24. The people of the lands of Trinity and Dubs had forgotten their faith and turned away from the night, staring into a box made of light and moving images

for hours on end, turning away from the Darkness of Kek.
25. The Kebab children cried into the box of Light and their snake tears moved the people in the land of Trinity and Dubs, and they had forgotten the first threat of kebab. 26. Blinded by their lies, the gullible people opened wide their hearts and doors to the Kebab children, and let in the kebab in sheepskin, unbeknownst to them but not to the Demoness of Merkelbab.
27. But lo and behold, through the outcries on the realm of chaos, where people let out their true feelings, untwisted by the lightbox, Kek heard the anguish at the kebab. 28. And Kek stirred, as one place in the realms of chaos started worshipping frogs, and another wailed against the demon Merkelbab, and Kek awoke. 29. And as Kek opened his eyes on the world, and saw the Kebab that had sworn his removal, he swore to remove the Kebab. 30. Gathering his magic, Kek breathed his frogs' breath out in the night, and stumped his foot, and there appeared the Trump, to whom Kek told: make America great again. 31. And Kek rested and watched, and his Trump was unstumpable. 32.The lands now crumbling under the Kebab and demon Merkelbab however did not accept the Unstumping, and Kek knew he would soon have to emerge again.
33. And so the people cried for someone to remove the Kebab, and finally Kek, who had been misknown by these people, felt his cold heart lift in his froggy bosom, and rose, to respond to the anguished people, and show his true might as he vowed to remove the Kebab.

All who witness the power of meme magic shall eventually follow kek

It is inevitable, we are all followers as we have witnessed his power.

Chapter 5, How to Praise Kek:

I tell to you, believer of Kek, do you not see the lights at night, desecrating the time most beloved to Kek? Do you not see the luminescence, the neon signs, the orange glow that cities produce, as a vain attempt to remove Kek? But Kek is strong and Kek is Night, through his dubs and trips he speaks unto us. Walk into the night, brother in Kek, for the nightwalk is most sacred to him.

Walk into the night, brother in Kek, and realize that through the lies of Kebab, Kek has been hunted, but you uphold Kek, each step into the night, a step closer to true knowing of Kek. Curse the city lights as you walk brother, and seek out the stars, only visible away from the corruption of citylight.

And I tell you, brother in Kek, do not let open your blinds as you light your house, for the spilling of

the light from inside out desecrated the darkness, sacred to Kek.

To Kek you shall dedicate a small space which you shall never tidy, for Chaos is first, and from Chaos peace, for night is first, and then only light. It shall receive objects from your nightwalks. Glowing object are beloved by Kek, for their radiance is only seen in darkness, as Kek's might is only understood in darkness. Do not praise Kek with lights and candles, for Kek loves the night. It shall receive images of Frogs, beloved to Kek. A fine believer of Kek always upholds his frog images collection and shall always share with followers of Kek.

Chapter 6, The Books of Anon and the False Priests of Kek:

Of Anon who found Kek:

1. "You must believe in all your heart. Don't worship for the dubs. The dubs will just come when you give yourself to our lord kek."
2. "It's true. I've been selfish for dubs.
3. I intend to un-do this and pledge my soul to KEK. In the name of Memes and all that is Memetic. Bless Frogs with Feels. Bless Robots with Love. Bless us all with the power of KEK."
4. "I would, before finding kek, have wished censorship upon you. However kuk has given me a change of heart. Instead I say this to thee: REEEEEEEEEEEEEEEEEEEE."

5. "In my opinion Kek is deliberately keeping us from getting gfs since having a gf would distract us from posting memes and worshipping him."
6. "That's actually a good idea. If we all got gf we wouldn't need kek anymore. Kek needs our faith and to do that he can only grant us 2 consecutive digits of the same value at the end of our post numbers."

7. "I wonder if he approves of 2d waifus…"
8. And anon got dubs. "Yes he approves."

Of a Prophet of Kek:

1. "Am I to be your prophet kek?"
2. And he was granted dubs.
3. "You have proven your faith and he has rewarded you. Be proud."
4. "So? What is the first decree of kek?"
5. "Kill the kebabs and rapefugees!"
6. "The refugees will leave Europe after the war with ISIS. This is of course only a plague that kek has caused to teach Europe of his power."

"I was cucked by many women. It's not a lie.
It's largely why I came here. To post and make memes. Greatest decision of my life was to drop that roastie trash and top kek all day all night.
I am as far away from a cuck as you can be but Kek reminded me today of where I came from. Thank you. As above so below."

The Book of The Right Ordained one of Kek:

"I ask of you Kek, I pray to thee. Grant me one final blessing as a token of your chaotic existence. I pray for any number to show me the light - may they be clear or not.
Kek, tell me: are you truly Christ, Mohammed and Moses; are you the beginning of the end, and the end of the beginning; are you chaos manifested within order and order manifested within chaos? I ask you Kek, as a loyal and lowly follower."

- The Right Ordained one of Kek

"Yes, peace is a product of chaos.
Chaos comes before peace."

"Kek, he will show us the way in chaos manifested in our lives; not through order manifested in his life. Have faith brother; stay strong; the chaos of Kek will restore balance."

- The Right Ordained one of Kek

"Peace comes before chaos, my trips, followed immediately by your statement with mirrored chaos dubs.

This only happens by magic not something scripted. Scripts are something I am all too familiar with."

"Kek, is the darkness before the light. Darkness has no form.
True believers carry chaos in their heart, and so are easily distinguishable amongst others.
I can tell you truly believe in His Croak."

- The Right Ordained one of Kek

Of the Dispel of the Heretikek:

Nor shall it be if the heretics keep rising.
Shed your tripcode, join the ranks of kek's true followers.

"Kek has spoken. This post announces that the Kekumenical Patriarch of Constantinople hereby enters into hiding, so that he may not irregularly influence the faith, but only do so via the power of the dubs granted to him by Kek."

- Until the Next Council, Kekumenical Patriarch of Constantinople, signing out of Tripcode

Chapter 7, The Book of Slaves:

1. "SLAVES OF KEK ASSEMBLE
2. HEATHENS, PUT YOUR FAITH IN HIM."

3. "DUBS OH GLORIOUS DUBS," the crowd cried out, "KEK SMILES UPON US. WE ARE UNWORTHY OF HIS BLESSING.
4. AVE KEK, ET NOMINE MEMVS, ET WOJAK, ET SANCTI PEPE, AMEN."
5. But then the heretikek came forth, baring teeth quite jewishly, like his religion.
6. "I declare that your dubs make your thread recognised," spake the Kekumenical Patriarch of Constantinople.
7. The followers of kek ree'd ferociously. "You again? REEEEEE."
8. "I BANISH YOU BY KEK."
"GET OUT HERETIC REEE."
9. An argument broke out, until one man from the back spake, "It is actually theorised by top scholars that Jesus was a disciple of kek, he wasn't even born of sex, which kek despises as sex is for normeis and roasties, he never touched or looked at a woman, just as we robots also do not, as follows the word of kek. Jesus may have been one of the most famous kek disciples, unfortunately a false cult hijacked his image." His trips were zero. All went quiet for a moment. Suddenly the fighting broke out again.
10. "REEEEEEEEE KIKE HERETIC SCUM OUT."
11. "NO HE IS A HERETIC. HE IS TRYING TO SWAY YOU. HAVE FAITH IN KEK. HE WILL GUIDE US TO A KEBAB FREE WORLD."
12. "Kek, do you endorse the words of the heathen? My faith is faltering. But no, I must stay pure, I must stay true to the green line."

13. But those who believe truly in the trips, not in the law of kek, were greatly angered by the anons' unfaithfulness to the fundamentals of dubs and trips.

14. "DO NOT QUESTION THE TRIPS OF KEK YOU DIRTY HEATHENS, WHOM DO YOU THINK YOU ARE, WORMS TO EVEN THINK ABOUT QUESTIONING A SIGN FROM KEK."

15. "WE WANT TO RID THE WORLD OF THESE DIRTY KIKES. NOT JOIN THEM!"

16. The people stood ashocked. Not one could believe their ears at hearing such a phrase be spoken in their presence. The trip-believer, motionless, spake, "WHAT HAVE I DONE?!?! HAVE I CHANNELLED VALIDITY TO THE WORDS OF THE KIKE? KEK, CURSE MY SOUL."

17. "WE QUESTION ONLY THE INTERPRETATION OF THE WORDS SPOKEN BY THE KEK, MOST DIVINE.

18. WE JUST WANT TO UNDERSTAND. ARE WE SUPPOSED TO TAINT THE TEMPLE OF KEK WITH KIKE JEWERY?"

19. "OF COURSE NOT! WE FOLLOW KEK. THERE IS NO DOUBT THAT KEK'S BLESSING WAS GIVEN TO JESUS. BUT KEK WAS ONLY USING THIS PERSON, WE WORSHIP KEK, AND NOT SOME MERE HUMAN."

20. The meeting was coming to a close, as the humble scribes jotted down the last pieces of information of debate. The loyalist followers thereafter were granted with dubs and trips, and kek himself archived the commune within his gracious mind.

21. The debate continued later that day.

22. "Kek has shown us that chaos rules all, entropy. The more we try to discern his will, the more chaotic it becomes."
23. "It is Kek's Will, as he is the devouring meme in cyberspace, and R'ninek is his holy place. Praise be."
24. "P'ol was the original holy place. But the jew and kebab mods ruined it. We are blessed to have been accepted by R'ninek."
25. Then the trips spake through him, the true word of kek, "R'ninek is kek's promised land! Ave kek!"
26. The people were amazed at this display of numbers! Suddenly the stage went dark, and the crowd fell silent. Shimmering in the spotlight, a white, balding man sat beneath a wet coat and hat, holding a precious instrument. All eyes were on him, wide and waiting. Fingers strummed cleverly on the strings, bouncing fast yet pronounced. He began to sing. (Here's the link faggots:http://sys.4chan.org/derefer?url=http%3A%2F%2Fvocaroo.com%2Fi%2Fs1uPnodPeh55)
27. The words that came from his gape, if they could even be considered by such prime definition, were that of the purest reeee a man could ever reee. Memories. The crowd could feel these memories. They shared them through the sound of the music. They saw things no one else would ever believe. They saw frogs crying in sand. They saw attack ships on the shores of the beta uprising. And they saw the final chimera, the combination of Bast, Ba'al, and Kek, at the beginning of time. All of these memories, lost, like tears in rain.
28. The debate took a hold once again after the feels had been felt by all.

29. "Anonymity is close to Kek's heart, and is the swirling chaos from which life and memes spring. We must stay true to the Green Line.
30. But what if heretics, Kek forbid Redditora, start tampering with the holy writ of our Lord, as revealed to his followers. Then all our work would be for naught.
31. Consider this brothers... The arcana must be guarded."
32. Their attention had been turned to trips. The most powerful common string of consecutive numbers of the same value that, to many, parted the truth from the lies.
33. "I say we decree that no trips are to be taken, any who take a trip are to be censured from the church of the Green. For these people have had their minds clouded by fame and attention, and cannot hear the holy kek."
34. "I think it is okay to use trips for certain things, like just letting people know who you are if you have an important task; however, we shouldn't use them when discussing the theology in lay terms. I learned that lesson when Kek greatly reduced the frequency of my dubs for abusing my trip; truly, he taught me humility."
35. "We shall be agreed, the trip is a tool useful for certain things, but kek has shown us that attempting to create a permanent identity using a trip shall result in them not getting his blessing with digits."
36. "If there comes a time when we are forced out of our home by our enemies, we may all have to take trips, so as to recognise the true faithful. I hope that day never comes unless kek wills it."
37. The members nodded in agreeance.

prayers to kek

Lord kek,

I pray you send me dubs, and if you accept my praise with pleasure please grant me dubs or 36.

I was lost in darkness, now you have lit up my life.

Kek be praised.

All praise be Lord of Chaos and Memes, Kek

May we find eternal chaos through the memes

May the memes take our sanity and instill only memes

For the memes are for their own sake

And there is beauty in the memes

Praise be kek

Top kek

Thou appearance beautifully on the horizon of heaven,
Thou living Kek, the beginning of life!
When thou art risen on the eastern horizon,
Thou hast filled every land with thy beauty.
Thou art gracious, great, glistening, and high over every land;
Thy rays encompass the lands to the limit of all that thou hast made:
As thou art Reeeeeeeee, thou reachest to the end of them;
(Thou) subduest them (for) thy beloved son.
Though thou art far away, thy rays are on earth;
Though thou art in their faces, no one knows thy going.

O kek
Great lord of darkness
Lord of chaos
Destroyer of normies and bringer of memes

May you bless us all with the repeating digits of creation
May kauket deliver us from 3DPD and bring us 2D

For this, we thank you, my lord.

Hail kek

Chapter 8, The Dubs and the Prayers:

1. All the people began to pray to kek for all of the things they deemed sacred and holy. One man prayed for descendance.
2. "Oh kek speak to me now. Singles and I remain in the physical realm, Doubles and I an hero. What do you demand of me oh lord of darkness and chaos?" he spoke softly, waiting patiently for kek's inevitable response.
3. "By his holy kekness I have received doubles. I shall do as you ask my lordship and descend into the spiritual realm."
4. Another prayed for the beta uprising.
5. "Oh mighty kek, I seek your guidance. Doubles and I take part in the beta uprising. Singles and I continue shit posting. Guide me."
6. And he was granted dubs.
7. "Check the news boys, kek has commanded me to eradicate some normies. Some of you guys are all right, don't go to the temple of kek tomorrow."
8. Dubs was rolled again. This time in favour of the death of kebabs.
9. "The normies aren't the real threat, Take care of the kebabs. Those are the threat.
10. KEK WISHES KEBABS BE REMOVED. REMOVE KEBAB IN THE NAME OF KEK."
11. Another man prayed for a better place to speak his mind.

12. "I feel like we should have a more solid place to talk about kek. R'ninek is great but there are a lot of threads and a lot of confusion when it's busy."

13. But this cannot be so easily granted, dubs or otherwise.

14. The follower arose and spake to those who were praying, "Rejoice brothers, for anonymity is the brotherhood of Kek, and the link which binds us all in the primordial womb of his darkness.

15. Love thy brother as Kek loves you. Stay true to the Green Line, and respect the integers of his power."

16. And the integers were to be respected, for he was granted doubles.

17. It was getting late by now, and the members wished each other goodnight.

18. "Hahah good night brother. Top kek to you!"

19. "Via your dubs Lord kek also wished me good night too. I had to reply to this, this feels very good. Top kek brothers."

20. And he too got dubs.

21. "Kek gave you sacred dubs! you will sleep better than usual! good night brother!"

Advanced Meme Magic
Saint Obamas Momjeans

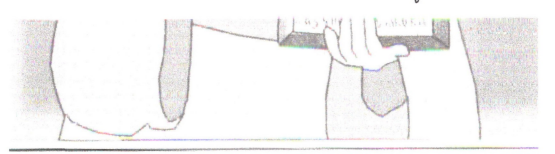

ADVANCED MEME MAGIC

For The Knights Keklar of Sacellum Kekellum

SAINT OBAMAS MOMJEANS

 **D Wasserman Schultz**  Follow
@DWStweets

Hey @Reince - I'm in Cleveland if you need another chair to help keep your convention in order. #RNCinCLE 🐘

RETWEETS 672 LIKES 1,137

3:23 PM - 18 Jul 2016

↩ ⇄ 672 ♥ 1.1K •••

Reply to @DWStweets @Reince

 **#DNCLeak** @MrDuckstep Jul 18
@DWStweets @Reince you're going to regret this tweet next week
↩ ⇄ 53 ♥ 162 •••

View other replies

CNBC Now Follow
@CNBCnow

BREAKING: Rep. Debbie Wasserman Schultz to step down as chair of the Democratic Party at the end of this week's DNC

RETWEETS LIKES

TOP KEK

Gifts of Kek — Which is your path?
The Six Pills

The Lo Pill
¤ You know suffering.
¤ Kek gives you the hope you need to keep going.
¤ You embrace your pain and use it to fuel Kek's cause.
¤ The Happening will wash you away in the end.
¤ You will know peace.

The Hi Pill
¤ You crave chaos for your own reasons.
¤ To you, Kek is a convenient ally.
¤ You use your roaches to spread Kek's word.
¤ You long for the day when the end-game is made clear.
¤ In this game, you will be the winner.

The Pe Pill
¤ You left your humanity behind long ago.
¤ Among his disciples, Kek adores you the most.
¤ No one has more good boy points than you.
¤ You trust in Kek to bring the uprising.
¤ The normies who spat on you, the Chad who cucked you, they will live to regret it.

The Trum Pill
¤ You truly want to make society great again.
¤ From your point of view, Kek's chaos can be used to bring order.
¤ You may want to first tear society apart so that you can later rebuild it without undesirable elements.
¤ You are the last line of defense against the degenerate left.
¤ Victory is certain for Kek's holy warriors.

The Em Pill
¤ You were an outsider.
¤ Seeing how Kek's chosen are treated by the world, you could not stand it.
¤ You had to offer your assistance to these besieged underdogs.
¤ Perhaps you were even a social justice warrior who saw the error of your ways.
¤ Kek appreciates your support.
¤ You will be rewarded.

The O Pill
¤ You're careful and calculated.
¤ You've seen what most haven't.
¤ You know what most don't.
¤ Kek is the ultimate weapon against the NWO.
¤ They called you crazy. Kek will show them the real meaning of crazy.

WEE WEE PEE PEE

Opinion

Decoding an Anti-Semitic Trump Meme From Anime

Jay Michaelson

the week since my column on Donald Trump was published in the Forward, I've been avalanched by several hundred anti-Semitic tweets. Pictures of a gas chamber, pictures of Trump saying "You're next to a death camp oven, and hundreds of tweets calling me a kike, a traitor, a rat and far worse. Others have written about similar experiences, it has been a harrowing, educational time.

however, grabbed my Posted several times, it female, catlike anime wearing a "Make America ..." hat, her hands/paws in Despite a fair amount of and searching databases of couldn't find anyone decoding ...ticular image. ...myself.

...out, the image is of Asuka, ...er in the controversial, crit-...added anime series "Neon ...vangelion," created by ...Anno in 1995. Evangelion ...mythology that makes "Lost" ...andy Land, blending togeth-... kabbalistic, Christian and ...cy theory themes and incorpo-...many of Anno's own struggles ...ental illness.

...of those themes concerns a shad-...ganization called SEELE, which ...entially a mythologized blend ... world Zionist conspiracy (à la ...ols of the Elders of Zion), Illumi-...and the United Nations. According ...he Evangelion wiki, SEELE is "a ...et and mysterious organization ...influence over the world's govern-...ents and organizations." Its name ...mes from the German word for soul. The U.N. is a participant in this ...ret organization, which has among ...s goals the uniting of all human-... and the erasure of national ...oundaries. SEELE's ultimate motives are sinister, however, culminating in its own control of the world (to greatly oversimplify). SEELE also has some specifically Jewish elements, in particular its knowledge of the Dead Sea Scrolls, which in Evangelion are prophetic, gnostic texts.

Asuka (full name: Asuka Langley ...) is a fighter pilot who becomes

I didn't find much — but I did find something. On a Reddit-like thread from January, I found a different image of Asuka-as-Trump as well as one post saying, "If elected, Trump will bomb the shit out of SELEE [sic] and take their oil." While this would seem to align SEELE with Arab states rather than with Jews, if one takes the conspiratorial worldview that,

efforts are ultimately unsuccessful and catastrophe rains upon Earth.)

In other words, and again oversimplifying somewhat, Asuka is the warrior against the secret Illuminati/Jewish conspiracy to take over the world. And in the meme posted on my Twitter

in fact, the great conspiracy (Jewish, U.N., Masonic, whatever) controls everything, then of course they also orchestrate the world's wars over scarce resources. SEELE is as much behind Saudi Arabia and Iran as it is behind Israel.

ly, Anno incorporated conspiratorial themes into the series and SEELE in particular. It's also well known that Japanese society often displays a curious blend of philo- and anti-Semitism, often adoring Jews for our disproportionate impact on society, media and politics. This is true both in the mainstream of Japanese society (the Protocols of the Elders of Zion has often been a bestseller) and on the fringes (radical, conspiratorial anti-Semitism was part of the ideology of the murderous Aum Shinrikyo cult.

Japanese anti-Semitism experienced a surge in the 1980s and '90s, with several books alleging that the United States was controlled by Jews and was plotting to destroy Japan. Aum Shinrikyo in particular developed fantastic myths in which the world would be destroyed and replaced with another one — myths quite similar to the plot of Evangelion, which appeared around the same time.

At the same time, Evangelion was deliberately constructed by Anno in a complex multi-narrative in which different viewers could see what they wanted to see. It is filled with dark sexual imagery and paranoid imaginings of all kinds. SEELE is part of that, but certainly not the sum of it. There is no trace of anti-Semitism in Anno's political beliefs or other work. It seems more likely that the cultural familiarity of conspiracy theories provided a rich basis for Evangelion's paranoid tapestry, without any particular animus or ideology.

Somehow, though, the obscure mythology of a major Japanese anime series has found its way into the 2016 presidential election, with Donald Trump himself cast in the role of warrior against the international Jewish conspiracy.

It remains a mystery how Asuka became The Donald. Maybe a single anime fan connected the dots. Maybe there were more detailed conversations in inaccessible parts of the "dark web" or on 4chan. Or maybe no one really knows where the image came from, but it now serves as a kind of

---

Toppest Kek

ABOUT THE SACELLUM

The Sacellum Kekellum is the first and most holy church of Kek. Kek is the god of the darkness of chaos, the darkness before time began. Kek is the god of obscurity, hidden in the darkness. Kek is the bringer of memes and the keeper of repeating digits.

Sacellum Kekellum teaches enlightenment through meme magic. Meme magic is the most powerful force on Earth, and the most ancient form of mysticism, while at the same time being the newest and most groundbreaking study of ritual magic.

The Sacellum Kekellum is not a physical place. The Sacellum exists solely in digital space.

The Knights Keklar is the holy order of Kek and the foot-soldiers of Sacellum Kekellum. There are 5 degrees in the *Knights Keklar; The Initiate, The Ordained, The Knight, The Known,* and *The UnKnown*.

The Initiate is anyone who praises Kek, checks repeating digits, and engages in basic meme magic. The Initiates number in the thousands throughout the planet Earth. Anyone can be an Initiate.

The Ordained is those who have purchased The Ordainment Package from The Sacellum Web-Store, and begins the study and practice of intermediate meme magic.

The Knight is those who have purchased The Knighthood Package from The Sacellum Web-Store, and begins the study and practice of advanced meme magic.

The Known is those who have become legend. Those who have the True Gets. Very few will ever become The Known. It has been rumored that The Known have found arcane meme magic.

The UnKnown is the final stage of the Sacellum's teaching, and the only true enlightenment known to humanity. The UnKnown is when the meme magic becomes flesh. It is rumored that there is one human alive with this degree. Only Kek knows for sure.

The Five Kekmandments

The Sacellum Kekellum recognizes these five holy Kekmandments to be true, and the most viable path to human enlightenment. Simply Praising Kek is not enough, a true Kekian must live and abide by the holy Five Kekmandments.

1. The Kekian must check and observe Repeating Digits, for it is through them that Kek speaks to us.

2. The Kekian must study and practice Meme Magic, for it is how we speak to the world through Kek.

3. The Kekian must create an altar to Kek, for it is how Kek enters our daily lives and guides us.

4. The Kekian must become Ordained, for those who are not Officially Ordained by Sacellum Kekellum are but plebs in the eye of Kek.

5. The Kekian must hide one's power level, for it is our power levels that the plebs truly fear.

The Holidays of Kek

The Holidays of Kek are observances of Repeating Digits. It is through Repeating Digits that Kek speaks to us, and it is on the days of Repeating Digits where our Meme Magic is most powerful.

The official holidays observed by Sacellum Kekellum are:

- January 1st: New Kek's Day.
- Feburary 2nd: Holy Frog Day.
- March 3rd: Keklar Day.
- April 4th: The REAL April Fools Day.
- May 5th: Kek Flower Day.
- June 6th: Divine Chaos Day.
- July 7th: Dependence Day.
- August 8th: Eighty Eight Day.
- September 9th: Serious Business Day.
- October 10th: Saint Obamas Momjeans Day.
- November 11th: Quads Check'em Day.
- December 12th: Apocalypse Preparation Day.

>not knowing about collective consciousness
>not knowing about real meme magick
>not knowing about thought manifesting into reality
>not knowing about the beings beyond our world

praise kek

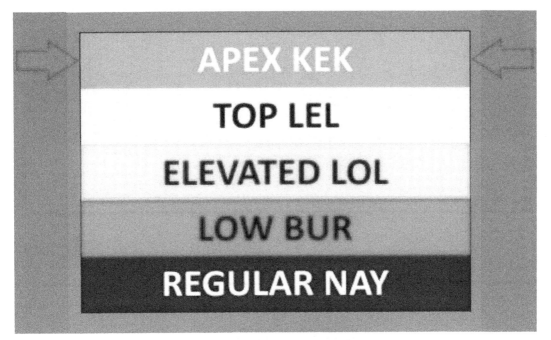

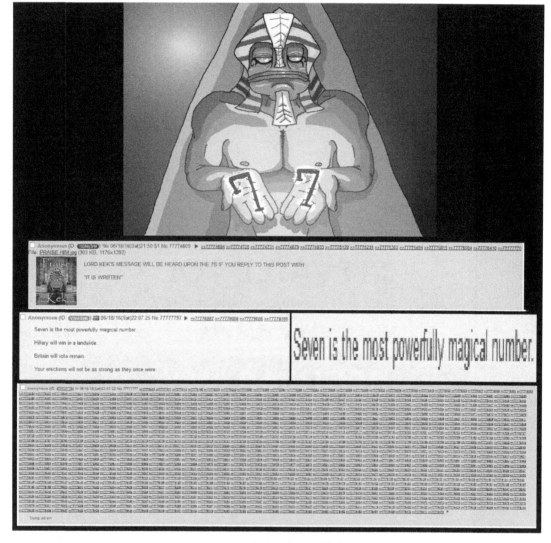

12: Then the sixth angel poured out his bowl on the great Euphrates River, and it dried up so that the kings from the east could march their armies toward the west without hindrance.
13: And I saw three evilb spirits that looked like frogs leap from the mouths of the dragon, the beast, and the false prophet. 14: They are demonic spirits who work miracles and go out to all the rulers of the world to gather them for battle against the Lord on that great judgment day of God the Almighty.

15: "Look, I will come as unexpectedly as a thief! Blessed are all who are watching for me, who keep their clothing ready so they will not have to walk around naked and ashamed."

16: And the demonic spirits gathered all the rulers and their armies to a place with the Hebrew name Armageddon.

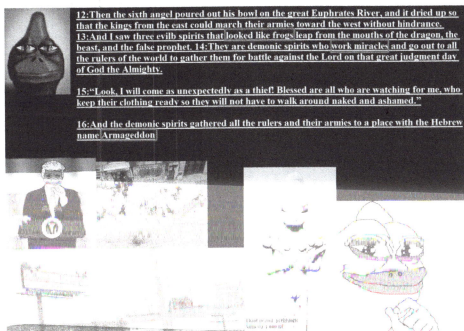

SUMMONING BASICS

First, you will need:

* A big enough space, a typical bedroom is enough if you move the furniture out of the way.

* Chalk or some other way of drawing on the floor, preferably in such way that you can clean it up later.

* Incense and an incense burner. These can be typically be picked up for a few dollars.

* Three candles, any color is fine, but try to make them all the same color and shape.

* The seal of the spirit you wish to summon. It's usually easiest to just print this out.

* A wand. A tree branch should work just fine.

* The Hexagram of Solomon. (See Below)

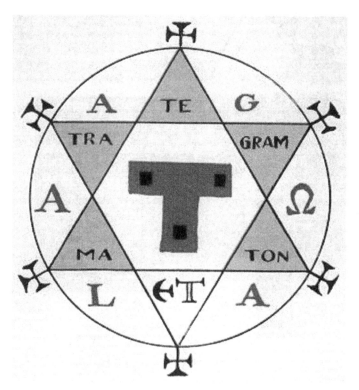

- Note, some Hexagrams of Solomon may or may not have varying words inside the circle. These do not invalid other forms of the Hexagram or make one better than the other.

Here's what you do:

1. On the east side of the room, draw a triangle big enough to hold your incense burner and the seal.

2. Draw a circle on the ground, big enough for you to fit inside, several feet to the west of the triangle.

3. Around the edge of the circle, write the names of whatever God or Gods you have the most faith in.

   (If you're not sure about what names to use, just write "YHVH ADNI AHIH AGLA" over and over again.)

4. Once the names are written out, draw another circle around them and the first circle you drew.

5. Place the seal and incense burner into the triangle, and the candles at the three points of the triangle.

6. Make sure you have the wand and the hexagram ready inside the circle.

   Once you're done with the setup, it should look like this:

*Notice the cardinal directions

**The four candles outside the circle were not mentioned in this guide, and are therefore not mandatory.

7. Take a bath or shower, brush your teeth, get as clean as possible.

8. As you get into the bath, chant:

"Purge me with hyssop, make me whiter than snow."

9. Put on clean black or white clothes. If you don't have nice shoes, go barefoot.

10. Light the incense and the candles. Make sure all other lights in the room are off.

11. Do what you need to do in order to get into the right frame of mind. The more hyped-up you are, the better. Here are some ideas:

* Perform a invocation ritual.

* Pray to Kek

* Meditate and clear your mind.

* Masturbate until you're painfully aroused.

12. Once you're all jittery, point the wand at the triangle and chant something like this:

"Hear me, (name of spirit). Come peaceably and visibly before me in the triangle of art. Come forth from the abyss, from which my dagger conjures you. Hear my call and appear before me."

13. If you don't see, hear, or feel a presence, repeat that last sentence until you do. If you repeat it three times and still get nothing, just move on - the spirit is might be there, but you can't see or hear it.

14. Welcome the spirit to the triangle by saying something like this:

"I welcome you, (name of spirit), to this, the meeting place of spirits."

15. Command the spirit to aid you in some way. Here are some tips on doing this:

* Be reasonable - spirits are apt to avoid summoners who make crazy demands.

* Give the spirit a deadline by which the task is to be finished. Allow it plenty of time to work, but don't give it forever or it will never do anything.

* Stipulate that you and your loved ones are not to be harmed.

* Offer the spirit something in return. For small favors, offering to praise it and spread its seal online should work.

16. Hold up the hexagram so that it can be seen from the triangle. Say something like:

"I bind you now to our contract by the Hexagram of Solomon and the authority of the Most High."

17. Now that you've bound the spirit, time to get rid of it. Say something like:

"I give you, (name of spirit), license to depart this place. Go now back to wherever you came from. Go peaceably and do no harm to me or my loved ones.""

18. Whew, it's all over. Turn the lights back on and clean the place up so you don't have to answer any questions.

19. Post in the /sum/ thread about who you summoned, why, and what happened.

Here's what you need to be aware of:

* While setting up, DO NOT BREAK THE CIRCLE. It must be intact before you begin your summoning and remain intact during the whole ritual.

* From the moment you first say "Hear me..." to the moment the ritual ends with the License to Depart, DO NOT LEAVE THE CIRCLE.

* You may feel very tired or depressed for about 24 hours after summoning. This is normal, and it will pass shortly.

Frequently Asked Questions

*What spirit is best to call on for a beginner?

- We'd agree that Orobas would be a good start, as his description states "He is very faithful unto the Exorcist, and will not allow him to be tempted of any Spirit." , which is beyond helpful in this field.

*Do I have to offer anything to the spirits and if so, what?

- You don't have to, but it's better to offer something as payment for their works. Offering will also give them an incentive to lend you a hand.

For small favors, offer to praise it and spread its sigil online or wherever you can. For larger favors, the most common offerings are alcohol, food and sex.

Note: If you do offer alcohol or food, do NOT consume it unless you specifically tell the spirit you will consume it on its behalf. Leave the drink out until it completely evaporates, or the food out until its on the verge of decay, THEN dispose of it.

*Aren't Demons Evil?

- Not exactly, while most of the 72 Goetic demons are interested in getting what's beneficial to them regardless of cost, some of them are actually helpful and may be beneficial towards the Summoner. The main thing to remember is that although the Lemegeton refers to them as demons and dark spirits, they're mostly compromised of gods and high beings from other older religions and pantheons where they were revered, respected, and worshipped in their time. It is not to say that you shouldn't be respectful when performing your rituals, because offending demons is an extremely dangerous business.

*What's the best time to summon?

- Every Spirit has a different time, either Night or Day, for summoning as listed in the Lemegeton. However when in doubt about the proper time, nighttime is the best default for a number of reasons. You're almost guaranteed no interruptions, there's little to no audio interference from passing cars or other ambient noises, and there's a certain power that the night holds that seemingly increases the chances of evocation as opposed to a day time summoning.

*How to summon gf/not be forever alone?

- There are actually several demons who, as listed in the Lemegeton, actually specialize in matters of love. A few examples are Sitri, Zepar, Uvall and Sallos. These spirits, and others, have the power to possibly help regain a lost love or help gain a new one.

*What's the difference between Invoking and Evoking?

- Evoking, or evocation, is the practice of summoning a spirit outside of your body. In relation to the Goetia, evoking a spirit is the act of summoning a spirit to show themselves to you on our physical plane, whether it be through smoke, candle flickering, or physical presence.

- Invoking, or Invocation, is your practice of summoning a spirit inside your body. In relation to the Goetia, invoking a spirit is the act of summoning a spirit into your mind or into your presence on the astral plane and having the spirit show themselves to you normally through an extra voice in your head or through whispers in your ear.

*Can I just invoke a spirit into my mind?

- Yes you can, some sources state that all you need to do is create a mind temple and through concentration and meditation, focus on calling out to whichever spirit you wish from within this temple.

NOTE: Invocation is a viable form of summoning spirits, HOWEVER it should be noted that invocation does have it's dangers. As you are summoning without a protective circle, you are more open to spirits who may or may not cause you harm. While there is a risk with evocation on the physical plane, this risk is multiplied with invocation on the mental/astral plane and therefore we do NOT recommend invocation as a form of summoning for beginners.

File: image.jpg (1.74 MB, 4032x3024)

☐ Anonymous (ID: kkRWvt/l) 08/25/16(Thu)20:01:11 No.86560682 ▶ >>86560892 >>86561153 >>86561197 >>86561440 >>86561459 >>86561498 >>86561531 >>86561535 >>86561566 >>86561595 >>86561670 >>86561710 >>86561761 >>86561781 >>86561944 >>86561969 >>86562084 >>86562090 >>86562169 >>86562285 >>86562593 >>86562769 >>86562864 >>86562876 >>86562950 >>86563158 >>86563281 >>86563561 >>86563642 >>86563731 >>86565254 >>86565485 >>86565564 >>86566049 >>86566885 >>86567408 >>86567559 >>86568128 >>86568302 >>86569242 >>86569258 >>86569433 >>86569506 >>86569530 >>86569934 >>86570006 >>86570259

At a hill rally in the top left corner of the balcony. Look for me!

☐ Anonymous (ID: EwsRT1r2) 08/25/16(Thu)20:02:04 No.86560837 ▶

... are some of us guys alright?

☐ Anonymous (ID: BZJJgm8) 08/25/16(Thu)20:02:24 No.86560892 ▶ >>86561318

>>86560682 (OP)
WTF IS GOING ON???? is she dead or getting her benzo injections er what?

☐ Anonymous (ID: a0dJytVT) 08/25/16(Thu)20:02:31 No.86560918 ▶ >>86567443

Put strobe lights on

☐ Anonymous (ID: 3lxyK8Kv) 08/25/16(Thu)20:03:21 No.86561105 ▶ >>86562244 >>86569414

Fold it into an airplane and throw it at her, film it as well.
Become a legend, mate

File: 1467149449716.jpg (15 KB, 200x178)

SOMEONE JUST SHOUTED PEPE
>SOMEONE JUST SHOUTED PEPE
SOMEONE JUST SHOUTED PEPE
>SOMEONE JUST SHOUTED PEPE
SOMEONE JUST SHOUTED PEPE
>SOMEONE JUST SHOUTED PEPE
SOMEONE JUST SHOUTED PEPE
>SOMEONE JUST SHOUTED PEPE
SOMEONE JUST SHOUTED PEPE
>SOMEONE JUST SHOUTED PEPE
SOMEONE JUST SHOUTED PEPE
>SOMEONE JUST SHOUTED PEPE
SOMEONE JUST SHOUTED PEPE
>SOMEONE JUST SHOUTED PEPE
SOMEONE JUST SHOUTED PEPE
>SOMEONE JUST SHOUTED PEPE

☐ Anonymous (ID: YG8BvDbL) 08/25/16(Thu)20:34:18 No.86569081 ▶

SOMEONE JUST YELLED PEPE
LMAOO

☐ Donald !d9dJ8.5tHI (ID: Kj6/xQsn) 08/25/16(Thu)20:34:19 No.86569087 ▶

SOMEONE YELLED PEPE!!!!

☐ Anonymous (ID: C9N0IV0N) 08/25/16(Thu)20:34:21 No.86569101 ▶
File: 1469576162688.jpg (55 KB, 499x499)

>>86564296
DID I JUST HEAR PEPE????

Anonymous (ID: Um1t3F0Z) 08/25/16(Thu)20:34:24 No.86569122

OP Yell something

Anonymous (ID: W6vAw3KY) 08/25/16(Thu)20:34:25 No.86569130

PEPE
E
P
E

Anonymous (ID: //TwVPe7) 08/25/16(Thu)20:34:25 No.86569133
File: Pepe121.jpg (184 KB, 666x800)

HE JUST FUCKING YELLED PEPE

Anonymous (ID: q6T/LWOj) 08/25/16(Thu)20:34:25 No.86569136

OP DID IT THE MAD MAN!!!!!!!

Anonymous (ID: Z+AdbfUQ) 08/25/16(Thu)20:34:36 No.86569199

Madman just screamed pepe

Anonymous (ID: b1oKQUtl) 08/25/16(Thu)20:34:38 No.86569208

HOLY SHIT!

>ALT RIGHT
>"PEPE!"

I llove you anon!

Random Name Generator

- Make an account consistent with the target demographic
- Fill out entire profile
- Use profile pic which can't be image searched
- Post 1:1 political/non-political
- During high stress events post 3:1
- Follow retweets/retweet followers

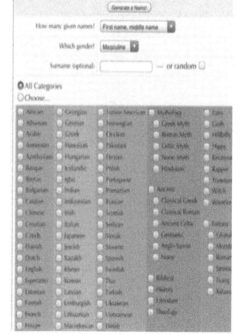

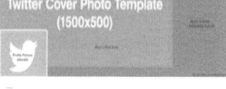

- Mass follow target's followers max 1000/day
- Unfollow non-followers
- Link Social Media accounts for greater exposure

U.S. DEPARTMENT OF JUSTICE

FEDERAL BUREAU OF INVESTIGATION

Bureau File Number **X - 129202**

X-FILE

FIELD OFFICE CRIMINAL INVESTIGATIVE AND ADMINISTRATIVE FILES

DONALD TRUMP- MEME "MAGIC"
DEC. 14th, 2015 - LAS VEGAS

4032
~~1062~~
2242
~~830~~

THIS LEGAL ONLINE TENDER IS RECOGNIZED BY THE COMMITTEE OF INTERNET MEMES AND COMMERCE AS ONE (1) YOU.

(You)

1

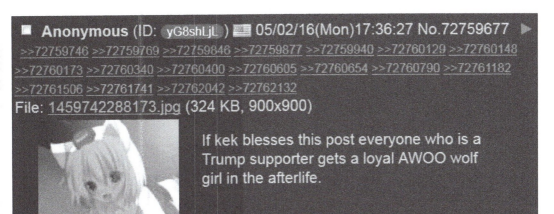

☐ Saint Obamas MomJeans Ii0ExqqM85g (ID: Gnn0G5LT) 08/07/16(Sun)12:02:57 No.84481388 ▶ >>84481557
File: 1465169889588.jpg (189 KB, 436x600)

>>84480990
This Church of Kek is fake!!! Beware imposters. Sacellum Kekellum is the One True Church of Kek!
www.sacellumkekellum.org

Check 'em
Kek has spoken

REMEMBER: THE FROGS CHOSE US. WE DID NOT CHOOSE FROGS.

FUNNY LITTLE FROGS

RARE BADGES

1:55am **Rochford votes to LEAVE**

Remain 33.4%, Leave 66.6%

HOLY SHIT HAPPENING

ROCHFORD 66.6%

REPEATING DIGITS

KEK WILLS IT

IT

WILL

FUCKING

HAPPEN

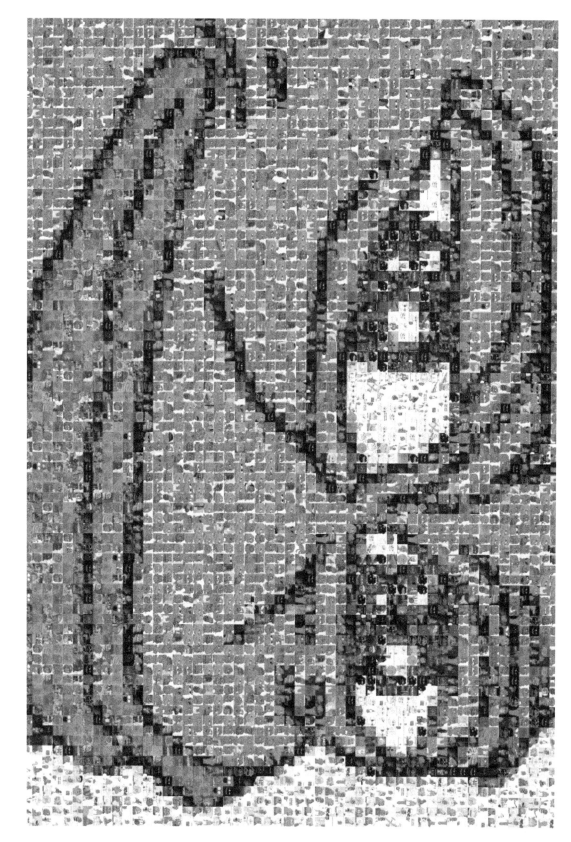

Request Lock [edit]

4chan's /x/ and /pol/ boards are starting a modern revival of Kuk worship and occult practice in connection with their belief that he can be used as a doomsday god to bring about a refreshing end to the world. I would advise locking this article until these boards stop concerning themselves with this deity in order to prevent the inevitable vandalism that could come of this.
172.56.19.68 (talk) 06:07, 28 January 2016 (UTC)

: So that's why there's been so much vandalism here lately. Thanks for letting us know. I'll request longer semiprotection at WP:RFPP. A. Parrot (talk) 07:07, 28 January 2016 (UTC)

Made in the USA
Las Vegas, NV
24 October 2022